GULLIVER

BEYOND

– contemporary writers apply the lessons learned by SWIFT'S TRAVELLER TO LIFE TODAY

EDITED BY PAUL BARKER

MARCEL BERLINS, JULIAN CRITCHLEY, CHRISTINA HARDYMENT, GERALD KAUFMAN, MILES KINGTON, GEORGE MONBIOT, CRISTINA ODONE, POLLY TOYNBEE

GULLIVERS TRAVELS

Ted Danson heads an impressive cast in this lavish new adaptation of Jonathan Swift's timeless classic. The film follows the journeys of Dr Lemuel Gulliver to strange and wonderful lands, inhabited by manikins, giants, immortals and hyper-intelligent horses. It counterbalances these adventures with an imagined portrayal of Gulliver's reception back home. These scenes are set in 1726, the year Swift's extraordinary story was published. Gulliver is disbelieved and (like Swift at the end of his own life) written off as mad. But his enemies are finally routed.

Also starring Mary Steenburgen, Edward Fox, Nicholas Lyndhurst, John Wells, Richard Wilson, Peter O'Toole and a host of other distinguished actors, *Gulliver's Travels* includes state-of-the-art special effects. The film was hailed as the 'television event of the decade' when it was broadcast in the US in February 1996, drawing a record-breaking audience of more than 56 million viewers. *Gulliver's Travels* is directed by Charles Sturridge (*Brideshead Revisited*), produced by Duncan Kenworthy (*Four Weddings and a Funeral*) and written by Simon Moore (*Traffik*).

Published in 1996 by Channel 4 Television, 124 Horseferry Road, London SW1P 2TX

Produced by Broadcasting Support Services to accompany the feature film *Gulliver's Travels,* an RHI Entertainment presentation in association with Channel 4 Television from Jim Henson Productions, broadcast on Channel 4 Television in April 1996.

Endpapers: (front) Gulliver on board ship, (back) Gulliver returns home, by French caricaturist Gavarni, 1862 (Mary Evans Picture Library)

ISBN 1 85144 160 3

Editor: Paul Barker Managing Editor: Paula Snyder
Designer: BIG-i, London Printer: Windsor Print
Distributed by Broadcasting Support Services

Broadcasting Support Services provides follow-up services for viewers and listeners and runs long-term helplines.

To help viewers follow up the issues raised by programmes, Channel 4 publishes a wide range of booklets, factsheets and edited transcripts, as well as organising telephone support services. You can also access Channel 4 programme support on the internet.
http://www.c4support.bss.org

For further copies, please send a cheque or postal order for £4.95
(made payable to Channel 4 Television) to:
GULLIVER AND BEYOND
PO Box 4000 London W5 2GH or Cardiff CF5 2XT

Contents

EDITOR'S NOTE

I have always been a great admirer of *Gulliver's Travels*. So I eagerly seized on Channel 4's suggestion to bring together a collection of contemporary essays which would emphasise Swift's continuing resonance and relevance more than a quarter of a millenium after Gulliver's adventures first appeared in print. Though Gulliver himself has become a kind of folk hero, I suspect that (apart from children's versions) Swift's extraordinary satire is more often praised than read.

I have been fortunate in my collaborators. Springing off from specific aspects of *Gulliver's Travels*, they have brought his strictures to bear on the society we live in today. It would be good to report that they brought in a verdict of 'Not Guilty'. But it seems we often fall into the same traps of pride, anger, greed and covetousness.

Sir Julian Critchley hears contemporary echoes in Swift's indictment of political venality. Cristina Odone and Gerald Kaufman contemplate today's religious and territorial quarrels – the equivalent of the great Lilliput-Blefuscu war between the Big-Endians and the Little-Endians. Polly Toynbee and Christina Hardyment find Swift's portrayals of old age and of self-indulgence uncomfortably close to the bone. Miles Kington notes that we are still vulnerable to pseudo-scientific panics.

George Monbiot, however, takes up the cudgels against the King of Brobdingnag's advice that politicians would be better advised to spend their time making two ears of corn grow where only one grew before. And, reflecting on the law then and now, Marcel Berlins thinks that Swift would be pleasantly surprised at how things have improved. (But then Swift was not easily placated and doubtless he would find other judicial targets for his arrows.)

The shape of this collection mainly follows that of *Gulliver's Travels* – from Lilliput through Brobdingnag, to Laputa and the country of the Houyhnhnms. It reproduces Swift's maps of his imaginary lands and relates these to the 'exploration culture' of the day. Each contemporary account is accompanied by the matching extract from the original. Other extracts are included in order to convey more of the flavour of Swift's satire. The illustrations mostly show how Gulliver has been portrayed down the years, as well as giving one interpretation of how the flying island of Laputa managed to stay up in the air. A final note puts Swift's life in the context of his turbulent times. He had a lot to be satirical about.

PAUL BARKER

WHY GULLIVER LIVES

PAUL BARKER *asks what gives Swift's story its continuing power*

GULLIVER is one of a handful of characters from English literature who are known to almost everybody, whether or not they have ever read the book. Others are Robinson Crusoe, Oliver Twist and Peter Pan. They have leapt out into the public imagination. All four have something in common. They are on their own against hostile surroundings and all are men or boys. The only female near-equivalent I can think of is Alice in her male-created wonderland. This may tell us something about the English.

The adventures of the famous four cast a new, ironic light on everyday assumptions: Robinson Crusoe on what we really need in order to survive; Oliver Twist on how we should treat the 'underclass' who, it seems, are always with us; Peter Pan on the cosy assumptions of our suburban lives.

But Gulliver is in a class of his own. Is that why we give him the blunt honour of always referring to him by his last name only, as if he were some kind of aristocrat of satire? (Few people, even after reading the book, remember that his Christian name is Lemuel.) *Gulliver's Travels* is astonishingly wide-ranging in its attack on the way we live. Many of these onslaughts are as vivid as the day they were written. They may have been aimed, sometimes, at particular abuses of the time. But Gulliver would not be alive and kicking hard, two and a half centuries after Jonathan Swift invented him, if the abuses he mocked didn't have close analogies today.

I was introduced early to one version of Gulliver. The first film I ever saw was the Fleischer brothers' animated *Gulliver's Travels.* (Like most adaptations, this meant only his first voyage, to Lilliput.) It was a pioneering attempt to rival Walt Disney. But Max and Dave Fleischer remain better-known for their cartoon shorts of Popeye and Betty Boop.

At my next birthday, my mother followed this up with a card game where each card showed a still from the Fleischer film. I could never understand the rules. But I liked to spread the cards out in the remembered order of the story, from Gulliver being found on the beach at night by Gabby, a comic night watchman (a Fleischer invention), with his flashing lantern. It is perhaps not surprising that, years later, the second or third book I ever bought with my own money was the book of the film.

This is one personal piece of evidence for the mysterious power of *Gulliver's Travels.* It is one of the rare stories that works both for children and for adults.

For children, I think this is partly because they respond to the recurrent preoccupation with size in Gulliver's best-known voyages – to the tiny Lilliputians and the giant Brobdingnagians. Being a great deal smaller than many of the people they come across (and hoping to do something about it) is at the heart of a child's experience. But, mostly, I think children respond because – in ways we can only be half sure of 270 years later – Gulliver's experiences are dredged up out of Swift's own childhood fears.

The voyages are by no means jolly romps. The cartoon versions, on film and in comic books, sell them short, turning venom into saccharine. The real Gulliver knows genuine fear and genuine revulsion. Like a child, he is often blamed unjustly. The Brobdingnagians and Houyhnhnms blame him simply for being a human. The Lilliputians, with even less justice, blame him for his good deeds.

At one level, the stories relate to a precise historical moment. Swift was writing in the era of some of the greatest English voyages of discovery. The locations of Swift's imaginary islands, on the maps he offered his readers, show the wondrous unknown regions of his day: the Indian Ocean and whatever lay to the south of it, and the unimaginably wide Pacific. It was a heyday for travellers and travellers' tales. In 1717, nine years before *Gulliver's Travels*, Daniel Defoe published *Robinson Crusoe*, which is usually thought of as the first English novel. Crusoe is based on Alexander Selkirk, who was set ashore on a South Pacific island during an expedition in which he quarrelled with his captain, then was rescued by the explorer-pirate, William Dampier.

This is the world of everyday terrors that Lemuel Gulliver travels in. But when you think back to Jonathan Swift's own life, you wonder what other terrors the story hides, and give it its strange force. Swift was a posthumous child, born after his father's death to an Anglo-Irish family. In his infancy, he saw little of his mother. Within a year of his birth he was amicably kidnapped. This is how he described it later, with his usual air of extreme detachment:

> *When he was a year old an event happened to him that seems very unusual, for his nurse who was a woman of Whitehaven, being under an absolute necessity of seeing one of her relations, who was then extremely sick, and from whom she expected a legacy, and being at the same time extremely fond of the infant, she stole him on shipboard unknown to his mother and his uncle [at whose house the Swift family lived] and carried him with her to Whitehaven, where he continued for almost three years. For when the matter was discovered, his mother sent orders by all means not to hazard a second voyage, till he could be better able to bear it.*

He saw little of his mother after that, being sent away to school and college till he was an adult.

In a sense, he was marooned for most of his life. Anglican families like his were top dogs in Ireland when it was under English rule. Or, more precisely, top horses (which is relevant to Gulliver's fourth voyage, among the Houyhnhnms). These were the people the Catholic Irish called the Horse-Protestants. But back in England they were not well thought of. They were only colonials. Swift spent most of his unhappy public career trying to balance between these two lives. In England he solicited his powerful friends for jobs (the only way to get them then). In Ireland (where the only job he could eventually get was as Dean of St Patrick's in Dublin), he always felt an exile.

He could never keep his fierce sense of irony under control. Politically he began by supporting the Whigs, and then he switched to the Tories. It did him no good. Swift was admired but never, I think, trusted. But his outsiderishness is one of the things that appeals to us now.

Swift had many psychological scars. His relationships with women can only be called perverse. He seems to have been fond of them, up to a point. But beyond that point he seems, from the surviving evidence, to have treated them either with cruelty or else as a special kind of baby. He couldn't forgive women for being as human as men. He was obsessed by the contrast between bodily beauty and other bodily functions. In his most notorious poem, parodying the languid elegies of the day, the lover explains why he has decided to abandon his mistress:

Nor wonder how I lost my Wits;
Oh! Celia, Celia, Celia shits.

Gulliver, like Swift, is a flawed hero. Many of Swift's faecal obsessions recur during Gulliver's adventures. (One critic speaks of Swift's 'excremental vision'.) As he tells Gulliver's story, Swift usually taunts men with their stupidity and cruelty; women are taunted for their ugliness and their sexuality. In the land of the Houyhnhnms, Gulliver is alarmed and disgusted when a Yahoo woman tries to seduce him. In Brobdingnag, he treats the giantesses who look after him – including the kind young girl he calls his nurse – like specimens under a magnifying glass, which in a way they are.

But today this obsessive streak helps to give Swift's writing its continuing power. You don't become the greatest satirist in the English language by 'coming to terms' (in social work jargon) with your problems. George Bernard Shaw was another Anglo-Irishmen with skeletons in his family cupboard. He said that, in his writing, 'I make my skeletons dance'. So did Swift.

Till quite recently, these obsessions – Swift's famous 'coarseness' – caused many of those who admired him to hunt for words of apology. James Joyce, an Irish writer from the other side of the horse-blanket, has since taught us that, even in literature, obscenity has a power of its own. But Swift retains the ability to shock.

When he wrote *Gulliver's Travels,* it was dangerous, and sometimes fatal, to mock monarchs, religions and politicians. This then had the power to jolt. Today much of this is the small change of television comedy. His misogyny is what brings you up short. If the book wasn't a classic, publishers would be making worried telephone calls to the author and suggesting tactful cuts, 'especially for the American market.' Tact is not Swift's line.

His satire is so much about the general human condition that almost all his targets have contemporary equivalents. When Gulliver puts out a dangerous fire at the imperial palace of Lilliput by urinating on it, thus saving the empress's life, he gets no thanks. Worse, he is threatened with death for high treason. He has broken a royal environmental ordinance against making water in the palace grounds. Originally, Swift may have been thinking of the poor return he got for pamphlets written in support of Queen Anne. Today your thoughts go to the dictatorial tone of other ordinances. In early 1996, the convicted murderer, John Taylor, met his death in Utah by firing squad. He had the condemned man's usual hearty breakfast. He also had a last cigarette. But, it was reported, he had to smoke this as he walked through the snow from his cell to the execution shed. In Utah it is forbidden to smoke inside any public building.

Children like the forbidden side of Swift. He is as uncensored as they are. *Gulliver's Travels* also has some of the power of a fairy tale: it conveys no simple moral message. In *Grimms' Fairy Tales*, for example, is it right that Cinderella's ugly sisters get their eyes pecked out by pigeons when they are acting as bridesmaids at her wedding to the prince? Or do right and wrong have nothing to do with it?

When Swift makes what at first appear to be moral points, he delivers them in a very enigmatic wrapping. For example, throughout his final voyage, he praises the Houyhnhnms for their perfect society. He shares their scorn for the brutalised Yahoos. How are we meant to take this?

The way these fabulous horses run their lives offers us an impossible ideal. There are no disputes, no over-indulgence. Sin has been abolished. (Sin in every sense. As in Lilliput, the local rule is that sex is only for procreation. Swift himself was childless. Scholars disagree over whether he contracted a secret marriage. They seem to be agreed that, if he did, it was a marriage only in name.) But the ideal of a world without conflict is a recipe for tyranny, as the French and Russian revolutions showed. Was Swift putting a layer of irony even over what seems to be his final moral recommendation?

Given the tenor of his other writings, he almost certainly was. The Irish dimension can never be forgotten in Swift. The warring islands of Lilliput and Blefuscu, divided by their ludicrous quasi-religious quarrel about eggs, may well echo England's many wars with Catholic France and

Spain. But they also echo England's angry involvement with Ireland. When the island of Laputa floats over its exploited colony of Balnibarbi, it may echo the way monarchs batten on their citizens. But it also echoes England's oppression of Ireland. When the Houyhnhnms claim that life would be perfect if only the loathsome Yahoos would be as civilised as they are, they reflect the attitudes of colonial rulers down the centuries. In particular, the English Protestant rulers of the native Irish.

Swift's most celebrated and enduring prose-satire apart from *Gulliver's Travels* is his pamphlet *A Modest Proposal for Preventing the Children of Ireland from Being a Burden to their Parents or Country.* It is the most ferocious dozen pages ever written in English. He suggests that, instead of neglecting and exploiting their Irish tenants, landlords should treat them as well as they would treat cattle. They should fatten up the children to be sold for food. This will cut down the numbers of Catholics, prevent over-crowding and give Ireland a new and profitable trade. (Swift had fought various campaigns to ease Ireland's disadvantages, but in vain.) The words corrode the page with their acid. Swift works out his proposal with the mad logic of Himmler deciding how to reach a final solution of the Jewish problem. The terrible truth is that, but for the taboo against cannibalism, the proposal made a lunatic sort of sense. The landlords who controlled the English parliament are shown the brutal logic of their policies towards Ireland.

Gulliver ends his voyages a sad, but not necessarily wiser man. He can't help seeing his wife and children as Yahoos when he gets back from staying among the Houyhnhnms. It wouldn't have helped him much, one suspects, if he could manage to see them as humans. When Gulliver told the King of Brobdingnag about the patriotic glories of English history, the king said, 'I cannot but conclude the bulk of your natives to be the most pernicious race of little odious vermin that nature ever suffered to crawl upon the surface of the earth.'

Robert Burns wrote that we needed the gift 'to see oursels as others see us.' In *Gulliver's Travels*, we see how Swift saw us. We can shudder, and be grateful. Like going out in the driving rain, such scorn brings with it a kind of exhilaration.

PAUL BARKER is a writer and broadcaster.
He is the former editor of *New Society*.

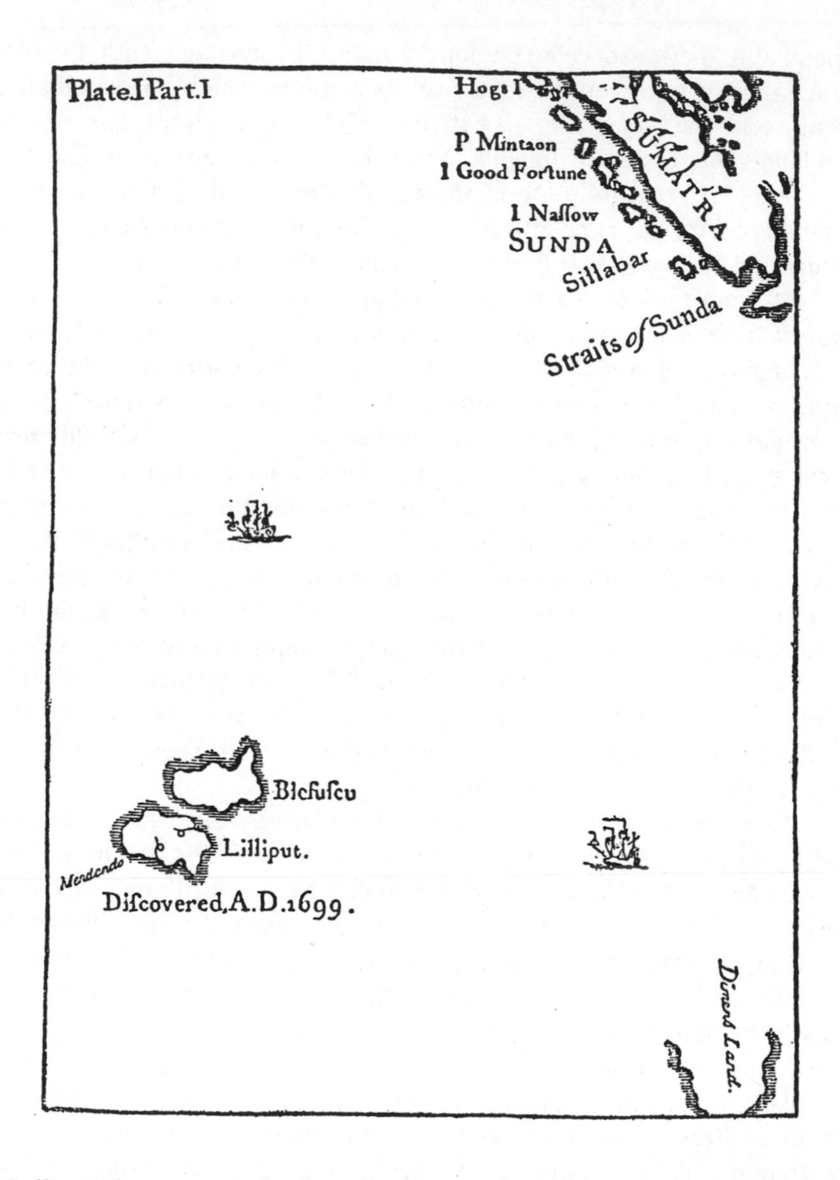

Gulliver's first voyage takes him to Lilliput, with its tiny inhabitants (about six inches tall). Lilliput is bitterly hostile to its neighbouring island of Blefuscu. Swift's map places the islands in the Indian Ocean, somewhere near the actual Cocos Islands, two low-lying coral atolls discovered by a British sea-captain in 1609 and uninhabited till the 19th century. The only part of Australia then known was Tasmania, shown on the map as Dimens Land.

Extract: Gulliver Awakes

In a famous early scene from his Lilliput adventure, Gulliver wakes up on the shore after being Shipwrecked.

I LAY DOWN on the grass, which was very short and soft, where I slept sounder than ever I remember to have done in my life, and, as I reckoned, above nine hours; for when I awaked, it was just day-light. I attempted to rise, but was not able to stir: for, as I happened to lie on my back, I found my arms and legs were strongly fastened on each side to the ground; and my hair, which was long and thick, tied down in the same manner. I likewise felt several slender ligatures across my body, from my arm-pits to my thighs. I could only look upwards; the sun began to grow hot, and the light offended my eyes. I heard a confused noise about me, but in the posture I lay, could see nothing except the sky. In a little time I felt something alive moving on my left leg, which advancing gently forward over my breast, came almost up to my chin; when bending my eyes downwards as much as I could, I perceived it to be a human creature not six inches high, with a bow and arrow in his hands, and a quiver at his back. In the mean time, I felt at least forty more of the same kind (as I conjectured) following the first. I was in the utmost astonishment, and roared so loud, that they all ran back in a fright; and some of them, as I was afterwards told, were hurt with the falls they got by leaping from my sides upon the ground. However, they soon returned, and one of them, who ventured so far as to get a full sight of my face, lifting up his hands and eyes by way of admiration. cried out in a shrill but distinct voice, *Hekinah degul*: the others repeated the same words several times, but I then knew not what they meant. I lay all this while, as the reader may believe, in great uneasiness: at length, struggling to get loose, I had the fortune to break the strings, and wrench out the pegs that fastened my left arm to the ground; for, by lifting it up to my face, I discovered the methods they had taken to bind me, and at the same time, with a violent pull, which gave me excessive pain, I a little loosened the strings that tied down my hair on the left side, so that I was just able to turn my head about two inches. But the creatures ran off a second time, before I could seize them; whereupon there was a great shout in a very shrill accent, and after it ceased, I heard one of them cry aloud, *Tolgo phonac*; when in an instant I felt above an hundred arrows discharged on my left hand, which pricked me like so many needles; and besides they shot another flight into the air, as we do bombs in Europe, whereof many, I suppose, fell on my body (though I felt them not) and some on my face, which I immediately covered with my left hand. When this shower of arrows was over, I fell a groaning with grief and pain, and then striving again to get loose, they discharged another volley larger than the first, and some of them attempted with spears to stick me in the sides; but, by good luck, I had on me a buff jerkin, which they could not pierce. I thought it the most prudent method to lie still, and my design was to continue so till night, when, my left hand being already loose, I could easily free myself: and as for the inhabitants, I had reason to believe I might be a match for the greatest armies they could bring against me, if they were all of the same size with him that I saw. But fortune disposed otherwise of me. When the people observed I was quiet, they discharged no more arrows; but, by the noise I heard, I knew their numbers increased; and about four yards from me, over against my right ear, I heard a knocking for above an hour, like that of people at work; when turning my head that way, as well as the pegs and strings would permit me, I saw a stage erected, about a foot and a half from the ground, capable of holding four of the inhabitants, with two or three ladders to mount it: from whence one of them, who seemed to be a person of quality, made me a long speech, whereof I understood not one syllable. But I should have mentioned, that before the principal person began his oration, he cried out three times, *Langro dehul san* (these words and the former were afterwards repeated and explained to me). Whereupon immediately about fifty of the inhabitants came, and cut the strings that fastened the left side of my head, which gave me the liberty of turning it to the right, and of observing the person and gesture of him that was to speak. He appeared to be of a middle age, and taller than any of the other three who attended him, whereof one was a page that held up his train, and seemed to be somewhat longer than my middle finger; the other two stood one on each side to support him. He acted every part of an orator, and I could observe many periods of threatenings, and others of promises, pity, and kindness. I answered in a few words, but in the most submissive manner, lifting up my left hand and both my eyes to the sun, as calling him for a witness; and being almost famished with hunger, having not eaten a morsel for some hours before I left the ship, I found the demands of nature so strong upon me, that I could not forbear showing my impatience (perhaps against the strict rules of decency) by putting my finger frequently on my mouth, to signify that I wanted food. The *Hurgo* (for so they call a great lord, as I afterwards learnt) understood me very well. He descended from the stage, and commanded that several ladders should be applied to my sides, on which above an hundred of the inhabitants mounted, and walked towards my mouth, laden with baskets full of meat, which had been provided, and sent thither by the King's orders, upon the first intelligence he received of me. I observed there was the flesh of several animals, but could not distinguish them by the taste. There were shoulders, legs, and loins, shaped like those of mutton, and very well dressed, but smaller than the wings of a lark. I ate them by two or three at a mouthful, and took three loaves at a time, about the bigness of musket bullets. They supplied me as they could, showing a thousand marks of wonder and astonishment at my bulk and appetite. I then made another sign that I wanted drink. They found by my eating that a small quantity would not suffice me, and being a most ingenious people, they slung up with great dexterity one of their largest hogsheads, then rolled it towards my hand, and beat out the top; I drank it off at a draught, which I might well do, for it did not hold half a pint, and tasted like a small wine of Burgundy, but much more delicious. They brought me a second hogshead, which I drank in the same manner, and made signs for more, but they had none to give me. When I had performed these wonders, they shouted for joy, and danced upon my breast, repeating several times as they did at first, *Hekinah degul*.

Extract: Advancement by Leaping & Creeping

The Emperor shows Gulliver *the tricks you have to perform to attain high political office in* Lilliput.

The Emperor had a mind one day to entertain me with several of the country shows, wherein they exceed all nations I have known, both for dexterity and magnificence. I was diverted with none so much as that of the rope-dancers, performed upon a slender white thread, extended about two foot, and twelve inches from the ground. Upon which I shall desire liberty, with the reader's patience, to enlarge a little.

This diversion is only practised by those persons who are candidates for great employments and high favour at court. They are trained in this art from their youth, and are not always of noble birth, or liberal education. When a great office is vacant either by death or disgrace (which often happens) five or six of those candidates petition the Emperor to entertain his Majesty and the court with a dance on the rope, and whoever jumps the highest without falling, succeeds in the office. Very often the chief ministers themselves are commanded to show their skill, and to convince the Emperor that they have not lost their faculty. Flimnap, the Treasurer, is allowed to cut a caper on the straight rope, at least an inch higher than any other lord in the whole empire. I have seen him do the summerset several times together upon a trencher fixed on the rope, which is no thicker than a common pack-thread in England. My friend Reldresal, principal Secretary for Private Affairs, is, in my opinion, if I am not partial, the second after the Treasurer; the rest of the great officers are much upon a par.

These diversions are often attended with fatal accidents, whereof great numbers are on record. I myself have seen two or three candidates break a limb. But the danger is much greater when the ministers themselves are commanded to show their dexterity; for by contending to excel themselves and their fellows, they strain so far, that there is hardly one of them who hath not received a fall, and some of them two or three. I was assured that a year or two before my arrival, Flimnap would have infallibly broke his neck, if one of the King's cushions, that accidentally lay on the ground, had not weakened the force of his fall.

There is likewise another diversion, which is only shown before the Emperor and Empress, and first minister, upon particular occasions. The Emperor lays on the table three fine silken threads of six inches long. One is blue, the other red, and the third green. These threads are proposed as prizes for those persons whom the Emperor hath a mind to distinguish by a peculiar mark of his favour. The ceremony is performed in his Majesty's great chamber of state, where the candidates are to undergo a trial of dexterity very different from the former, and such as I have not observed the least resemblance of in any other country of the old or the new world. The Emperor holds a stick in his hands, both ends parallel to the horizon, while the candidates, advancing one by one, sometimes leap over the stick, sometimes creep under it backwards and forwards several times, according as the stick is advanced or depressed. Sometimes the Emperor holds one end of the stick, and his first minister the other; sometimes the minister has it entirely to himself. Whoever performs his part with most agility, and holds out the longest in leaping and creeping, is rewarded with the blue-coloured silk; the red is given to the next, and the green to the third, which they all wear girt twice round about the middle; and you see few great persons about this court who are not adorned with one of these girdles.

At the Lilliput Court. (Hulton Deutsch)

HOW

TO GET ON IN

POLITICS

JULIAN CRITCHLEY *casts a cold eye on the greasy ladder to high office*

I HAVE been a Tory MP since 1959, leaving the Commons at the end of this parliament. I have served under five Conservative prime ministers, and have been advanced by none, although it is true to say that John Major (prompted by Michael Heseltine?) recommended my knighthood in the summer of 1995. My failure to make progress is not the subject of this essay, although it may have some bearing upon what I write. After Mrs Thatcher came to power in the Peasants' Revolt of 1975, I became an observer rather than a participant; by the time 'Dear John' replaced the Sun Queen in November 1990, I was too old for promotion. Had Michael

Heseltine won, he did promise me the governorship of the Falkland Islands, but who would want to live in bleak islands inhabited by sheep and undiscovered land mines, even at the price of a governor's cocked-hat and an old London taxi cab?

I have spent twenty five years watching the soles of the feet of my competitors climb the greasy ladder of promotion. How did they manage it? Most were not obviously more able than I. Roy Jenkins once told me that one Labour MP of his acquaintance (Anthony Greenwood) spent the better part of every morning writing in his own hand letters of congratulation to those of his colleagues who had spoken, however poorly, in the debate of the day before. With the help of his pen, Greenwood became a cabinet minister and a life peer. Enoch Powell once asserted that humbug was the essential lubricant of public life; I suggest that flattery, skilfully applied ('Minister, that was a most admirable performance'), can do no harm and much good. In the highly competitive atmosphere that permeates the Commons the admiration, both of friend and foe, is a valuable commodity.

In 1957, when Harold Macmillan, the son in law of a duke, presided as prime minister over our destinies, it was as well to be related to the Great Man, and it was truly surprising how many of 'the colleagues' could claim to be his kinsmen. Many were called 'Charlie' and wore cream silk shirts and frayed Old Etonian ties; many had slept with their kinsmen's wives and all had enjoyed what was called 'a good war'. The politics of the Great House, although much diminished since the end of Hitler's War, still existed. I did once manage to spend the weekend with the Nigel Birches in north Wales, but by that time Nigel and Harold were implacable foes, Nigel having resigned as a treasury minister over Harold's cheerful disregard of budget deficits.

The trouble was that I was the son of a doctor and the grandson of a railway worker and a gas company clerk. I was sometimes mistaken by the old things as the son of 'Critch', the Canadian adventurer who introduced greyhound racing into Britain, but I was obliged to tell the truth. We were not related. As a young man of 28 I had not served in the war, and the whips' office was closed to me; in those days it was run by the adjutants of good regiments and by junior officers with a 'good' Military Cross. As a public school boy and a graduate of two universities, I passed for white; but not white enough.

Margaret Thatcher seized power in the coup of 1975, when the back-bench 1922 Committee, under the leadership of the oleaginous Edward du Cann, conspired successfully to depose Ted Heath who, it must be said, had committed two cardinal sins: he had lost two elections running; and he was never sure of the names of his colleagues' wives. Margaret was at the time an unknown quantity; a noisy, opinionated woman with unfashionably right-wing views. She was quickly taken over by the far right and, being a woman of a domineering nature, soon set up a court of her own. *Life at the Court of Queen Margaret* became the title of many a journalistic article, mine included.

Margaret had a taste for handsome young men who combined the looks of Cecil Parkinson (one of her many party chairmen, now Lord Parkinson) with those of Humphrey Atkins (one of her chief whips, now Lord Colnbrook); sleek, youngish men who could have been under contract to Alexander Korda or to J Arthur Rank. They knew how to flirt and to flatter. They were careful never to take an argument too far. Mrs Thatcher, who was often as offensive as she was determined, claimed to enjoy a good argument, but she demanded the sort of loyalty that slips all too easily into shameless admiration. 'Is he one of us?' she would ask of colleagues, and was swift to nose out doubt. She saw herself as the leader of a counter-revolution, separate in some ways from her own government , continuously challenged by members of the 'old guard', impatient to the point of rudeness with the doubts of others.

As insecure as she was aggressive, she ran through a series of sycophants like Alfred Sherman (whom she knighted), a one-time machine gunner in the Spanish republican army, a Marxist who had turned his coat. She even knighted Larry Lamb, the editor of *The Sun*, in gratitude for his support. Alistair McAlpine paid court; Norman Tebbit played the 'heavy' until he, at long last, fell out with the prime minister during the 1987 election. Margaret had a taste for Jews such as Keith Joseph ('my mentor') and David Young whose political careers ended in failure. She saw Jews as firing on all twelve cylinders, outsiders in the sense that she was herself, the grocer's daughter from Grantham in a gentleman's party. But how best to cope with her?

She required her ministers to be on top of their jobs, but was not afraid to hector them in front of their colleagues, even the beautiful John Moore, a one-time favourite, briefly in charge of the health service (now

Lord Moore of Lower Marsh). She needed continual reassurance, which the more astute were never chary of offering. She basked in the admiration, both sexual and political, of her coterie ('I do like being made a fuss of by men'), and I can remember the pre-Westland Michael Heseltine telling me that he found her as unattractive as she was difficult. In short, Margaret demanded worship; she was boastful ('I have changed everything') and had little or no time for those with doubts, the sole exception being her long-suffering deputy Willie Whitelaw. Alastair Goodlad, John Major's chief whip, tells me that after Whitelaw there was no one left who had any influence over her. She had become a loose cannon.

But how best to attract her attention? The newly-elected backbencher could flatter her in the public prints (in which she was generally attacked) and, in return, would be sought out and asked for his advice. Every year at Chequers on Boxing Day a large lunch party was held to which 'Thatcherites', both from within and without Westminster, would be asked. The whips, under David Waddington and later Tim Renton, saw to it that promotion, at least at the lower levels, bore some relation to ability; at the top the cards were Margaret's to shuffle.

As Roy Jenkins once put it at lunch with me in Oxford, there is little point in praising a bad speech but every incentive to over-praise a good one. Despite Margaret's vanity, men are generally more susceptible to flattery than are women, except perhaps in the matter of good looks. Just as Ted Heath has been more than tardy in finishing his prime ministerial memoirs ('Ted can never bring himself to admit to having made an error') , so John Major appears to lack vanity, although he must be as vulnerable as anyone else to the supportive speech, the generous article, and the murmur of approbation. But one look at his cabinet suggests that he does not choose them for the same reason as did Mrs Thatcher.

No one who lacks vanity would stand for parliament. We talk of service, what we seek is admiration. Despite the tabloids, the letters 'MP' still stand for something. Despite Edwina Currie's in-house novels, we still are inclined to regard the House of Commons as the best club in London. We seek out the praise, not of those whom we may despise, or even of our peers, but of our intellectual superiors. (I would rather be praised by Europhiles like Ted Heath, Roy Jenkins or Ian Gilmour than by Eurosceptics like Bill Cash, Teddy Taylor or Christopher Gill.) Our vanity is such that our name springs out in heavy type from the newspaper we are reading. We flatter our superiors by agreeing with them. If it were not too late, would I consider seriously how best to flatter John Major? One can hardly refer to his decency, nor to his success. His equivocation over Europe does nothing for me. Perhaps I should make some reference to the soapbox that supposedly won him the 1992 election?

A friend in the whips' office, who shall be nameless, once told me of the extraordinary letters the whips would receive from MPs. Some would ask for titles (a request couched in flattering terms), others would bad-mouth their colleagues, hinting at extra-marital activity and, what was worse, disloyalty towards the leader and the party. 'We have more than our fair share of shits,' the whip complained. In Margaret's day flattery was at a premium; today, in duller times, one can only rubbish one's enemies to the lobby correspondents who buzz round the members' lobby like so many blowflies.

SIR JULIAN CRITCHLEY is the Conservative MP for Aldershot. His books include the political thriller, *HUNG PARLIAMENT*.

EXTRACT:

HIGH HEELS, LOW HEELS, BIG-ENDIANS & LITTLE-ENDIANS

A high official explains to Gulliver the threats to Lilliput. Politics is torn by the pointless rivalry between the High-Heel and Low-Heel parties (corresponding to the 18th century Tories and Whigs). Externally, there is the threat from neighbouring Blefuscu.

The animosity between the two islands is made worse by a row over which end eggs should be opened at. The Little-End and Big-End quarrel is Swift's parody of the disputation between Protestants and Roman Catholics over the significance of communion or mass: do the bread and wine only symbolise Christ's flesh and blood (consubstantiation) or do they miraculously become his flesh and blood at that moment (transubstantiation).

In the years before Swift's satire, the bitterest wars had been fought over such religious differences.

FOR, SAID HE, as flourishing a condition as we may appear to be in to foreigners, we labour under two mighty evils; a violent faction at home, and the danger of an invasion by a most potent enemy from abroad. As to the first, you are to understand, that for above seventy moons past there have been two struggling parties in this empire, under the names of *Tramecksan* and *Slamecksan*, from the high and low heels on their shoes, by which they distinguish themselves. It is alleged indeed, that the high heels are most agreeable to our ancient constitution: but however this be, his Majesty hath determined to make use of only low heels in the administration of the government, and all offices in the gift of the Crown, as you cannot but observe; and particularly, that his

Majesty's Imperial heels are lower at least by a *drurr* than any of his court; (*drurr* is a measure about the fourteenth part of an inch). The animosities between these two parties run so high, that they will neither eat nor drink, nor talk with each other. We compute the Tramecksan, or High Heels, to exceed us in number; but the power is wholly on our side. We apprehend his Imperial Highness, the Heir to the Crown, to have some tendency towards the High-Heels; at least we can plainly discover one of his heels higher than the other, which gives him a hobble in his gait. Now, in the midst of these intestine disquiets, we are threatened with an invasion from the Island of Blefuscu, which is the other great empire of the uni-

Blefuscu envoys offer peace. (Hulton Deutsch)

verse, almost as large and powerful as this of his Majesty. For as to what we have heard you affirm, that there are other kingdoms and states in the world inhabited by human creatures as large as yourself, our philosophers are in much doubt, and would rather conjecture that you dropped from the moon, or one of the stars; because it is certain, that an hundred mortals of your bulk would, in a short time, destroy all the fruits and cattle of his Majesty's dominions. Besides, our histories of six thousand moons make no mention of any other regions, than the two great empires of Lilliput and Blefuscu. Which two mighty powers have, as I was going to tell you, been engaged in a most obstinate war for six and thirty moons past. It began upon the following occasion. It is allowed on all hands, that the primitive way of breaking eggs before we eat them, was upon the larger end: but his present Majesty's grandfather, while he was a boy, going to eat an egg, and breaking it according to the ancient practice, happened to cut one of his fingers. Whereupon the Emperor his father published an edict, commanding all his subjects, upon great penalties, to break the smaller end of their eggs. The people so highly resented this law, that our histories tell us there have been six rebellions raised on that account; wherein one Emperor lost his life, and another his crown. These civil commotions were constantly fomented by the monarchs of Blefuscu; and when they were quelled, the exiles always fled for refuge to that empire. It is computed, that eleven thousand persons have, at several times, suffered death, rather than submit to break their eggs at the smaller end. Many hundred large volumes have been published upon this controversy: but the books of the Big Endians have been long forbidden, and the whole party rendered incapable by law of holding employments. During the course of these troubles, the Emperors of Blefuscu did frequently expostulate by their ambassadors, accusing us of making a schism in religion, by offending against a fundamental doctrine of our great prophet Lustrog, in the fifty-fourth chapter of the *Brundecral* (which is their Alcoran). This, however, is thought to be a mere strain upon the text: for the words are these; *That all true believers shall break their eggs at the convenient end*: and which is the convenient end, seems, in my humble opinion, to be left to every man's conscience, or at least in the power of the chief magistrate to determine.

BACK-YARD BATTLES

GERALD KAUFMAN *laments the trivialities that lead to war*

GULLIVER'S travels took him to a miscellaneous collection of small, daft countries, several of which were congenitally turbulent or bellicose. Swift records how, by 'an extraordinary stratagem', Gulliver prevented the invasion of Lilliput by the 'Empire of Blefuscu... an island situated to the north north-east side of Lilliput, from whence it is parted only by a channel of eight hundred yards.' The 'flying or floating island' of Laputa, which was 'exactly circular in shape' and 'ten thousand acres' in extent, was so subject to 'rebellion or mutiny' or to having its peace disturbed by 'violent factions', that its king felt required to adopt certain 'methods' for 'reducing them to obedience'.

The destinations to which Gulliver voyaged were, of course, potty little places which were, into the bargain, imaginary. Furthermore, all of the disturbances to which they were prone were invented by a satirist who lived more than 250 years ago. Such nonsenses could not possibly happen in real life and could not conceivably occur today; or could they?

Satire has survived into the 20th century and has been particularly prevalent on our cinema screens, where absurd hostilities can be not only imagined but depicted. Thus in 1933, in the greatest of all the Marx Brothers comedies, *Duck Soup*, Groucho presided as dictator over Fredonia, which went to war against an evil neighbour.

A quarter of a century later, in 1959, in *The Mouse that Roared*, Peter Sellers (as, simultaneously, grand duchess, prime minister and field marshal) led the minute nation of Grand Fenwick in an aggressive war against the United States. Grand Fenwick hoped for swift defeat by its giant adversary – thus, it trusted, becoming eligible for the customary aid provided by the USA for its humbled foes – but, regrettably, turned out to be the victor instead.

Fredonia and Grand Fenwick were, of course, as imaginary as Lilliput, Blefuscu and Laputa. In the real-life 20th century, genuine countries have been unlikely to be involved in comparable bloodshed; or have they?

It has to be admitted that war is so attractive and civil war so tempting that, in our lifetimes, wars and rebellions have taken place with as little apparent logical justification – especially seen in retrospect – as those mythical 18th century battles referred to by Swift and those imaginary 20th century conflicts purveyed on the silver screen. Pretty well every continent has been prey to such activities. Sometimes the objectives have, even at the time, seemed ridiculous. Even when the issues have been genuine and serious, outside observers have been astounded that the warring parties have been unable to settle their differences peacefully but have, instead, involved themselves in fighting which has resulted in destruction, suffering, refugees living in squalid camps and, worst of all, incalculable numbers of deaths.

India, sadly, has been especially prey to such conflicts. One such – intermittent and far from settled – relates to the wish of some Sikhs living in the Punjab to create a country which does not exist and has never existed, a longed-for land named Khalistan. Conflict between Indian armed forces and Sikh insurrectionists has led to terrible events. The beautiful and extremely sacred Sikh temple at Amritsar was seriously damaged, an event which created such fury that a Sikh member of her bodyguard murdered India's Prime Minister, Indira Gandhi.

In the north of that country conflict continues to this very day between India and Pakistan over the small state of Kashmir. To the outside world Kashmir used to be known for the heavenly beauty of its high mountains and verdant valleys. Now, most inhabitants of the outside world dare not venture there, for fear of being taken hostage by terrorist bands complicating a dispute which has split Kashmir into two parts, from which it is impossible safely to cross from one side to the other; has resulted in Muslim refugees fleeing in one direction and Hindu refugees fleeing in another; and has led to hundreds of thousands of deaths, together with rapes and mutilations.

In Africa what is, on the face of it, a preposterous squabble has continued for years, has provoked a war and has (like a number of other such local disputes) invoked the intervention of the United Nations. The argument is between less than 100,000 desert folk, the Sahrawis, and the government and armed forces of Morocco. The Sahrawis wish to achieve independence and self-government for a vast tract consisting mainly of golden sand, called the Western Sahara. The Moroccans – in no way, it should be said, influenced by the presence in the Western Sahara of considerable quantities of marketable phosphates – insist that the territory is theirs and express their intention of holding on to it. Result: fighting, casualties and miserable refugee camps.

Few of the minute nations of Central America have avoided squabbling with their neighbours. When Nicaragua was ruled by the left-wing Sandinistas, nearby countries – mostly with right-wing governments – did their best to overthrow the Nicaraguan regime. They, in their turn, were destabilised by the Sandinistas. Only Costa Rica – stable, democratic and secure enough to have voluntarily disbanded its army – escaped involvement and, indeed, tried to bring peace by mediation.

All of these, of course, are inhabitants of distant continents whose conflicts can arouse horror among Europeans for their sanguinary nature but can be accounted for, by those same aloof and arrogant Europeans, as due to the excitable national characters of those involved.

Yet Europeans, too, are no exceptions from such horrors. The most obvious example is what was once Yugoslavia, a country which even when united was neither politically nor economically powerful. Once the binding strait-jacket of communism was removed from Yugoslavia's varied ethnic and religious groups, they fell to fighting and persecuting each other as though they had been awaiting the opportunity for generations, if not centuries. Out of this maelstrom arose republics whose very existence, in logical terms, was farcical. One was even compelled to call itself The Former Yugoslav Republic of Macedonia; and there was severe dispute as to whether it actually contained any genuine Macedonians. The *casus belli* for these bands of warriors fighting each other may have appeared absurd to outsiders; but the suffering that followed rivalled any our planet had seen in the previous half-century.

A little farther east, the historic hatred between Greece and Turkey led in 1974 to the invasion by the Turks of the newly independent country of Cyprus, the majority of whose population was of Greek origin. The world did nothing while countless Cypriots were killed, their homes were grabbed by settlers, and precious and priceless works of art were plundered and sold on the international market. The most recent consequence of Greek-Turkish enmity was the first near-war of 1996, involving warships and diplomatic mudslinging, over the tiny (its 10 acres far more minute than Gulliver's Laputa), barren, guano-covered and goat-ridden Aegean island of Imia (Kardak to the Turks). The claim of both Greeks and Turks is irrelevant to its human inhabitants, of whom there are none. One non-Greek, non-Turk diplomat commented, 'This is the kind of dispute that only a Turk or a Greek can understand.' A Greek spokesman suggested that the most sensible way to resolve the dispute would be to have a referendum among the goats.

We British, and our superior trans-Atlantic allies the Americans, can of course raise our noses in disdain over such trivialities; or can we? After all, it was Margaret Thatcher who, as blousily grandiloquent as the Grand Duchess of Grand Fenwick, in 1982 burst triumphantly into Downing Street to urge Britain to 'Rejoice, rejoice!' over the liberation of the perfectly pointless South Atlantic island of South Georgia from a rabble of Argentinian scrap-iron merchants. It was Britain under a Labour government which, in 1969, grandiosely sent a force of 300 paratroops to bring order, in Operation Sheepskin, to the scarcely noticeable Caribbean island of Anguilla which, 16 miles long and two miles wide, with no telephones, water mains, central electricity or paved roads, had ludicrously declared itself an independent republic after purporting to secede from the scarcely world-shaking group of islands which adopted for themselves the fancy title of the Associated State of St Kitts-Nevis-Anguilla.

The Americans have behaved equally idiotically in the Caribbean. In 1983 they sent a force to the communist-ruled island of Grenada, in order to rescue American students who were in no danger whatever. With no adequate maps, the US invaders were guided by holiday picture postcards. A special contingent was allotted the mission of safeguarding the island's governor-general who, up to the arrival of his saviours, was perfectly all right but then became a target of hostile fire. When his US rescuers withdrew, the governor-general's wife's jewels were found to have vanished with them.

The most demented of all recent operations in the Caribbean was the American expedition dispatched in 1989 to oust General Manuel Antonio Noriega, the totalitarian boss of Panama. Noriega took refuge in the diplomatic safe haven of the Vatican's ambassador, the papal nuncio. The Americans tried to blast Noriega out by blaring 'skull-splitting' round-the-clock rock music from a nearby car park. Even the American ambassador in Panama City recognised that his country had gone too far: 'We received a note from the nuncio protesting either the loudness of the music or the quality, I'm not sure which.'

Swift, thou shouldst be living at this hour.

GERALD KAUFMAN has been a Labour MP since 1970. A former shadow foreign secretary, he currently chairs the *National Heritage Select Committee.*

QUARRELLING *at* *HEAVEN'S* GATE

CRISTINA ODONE *wishes religion brought more love and less anger*

WHY is it that religion can raise men to greatness – but also reduce them to Lilliputian stature? Religion may bind men and women in a collective worship of transcendental truths, but these same worshippers all too often genuflect at the altar of sectionalism, spouting strident slogans of hatred. Ironically, it is in the very strength of religion that lies the seed of internal discord. For, if adherence to a set of beliefs yields the faithful an all-important, reassuring sense of membership from which they may draw great strength, it also fuels a sense of us-against-them which, as history shows, repeatedly erupts in vicious conflict.

The Jews of the Old Testament were the first to unite under the banner of the 'chosen people' – finding in this holy epithet the hope and courage to withstand their years of exile. But later, from the Christian crusade to the Muslim jihad, what was once a passport to heavenly rewards became an all too terrestrial fanaticism that spurred the believer into battle. Here, upon a field marked by prejudice, ignorance and fear, and issuing blood-curdling battle cries of 'Death to the Infidel!' the believer sought to wreak total destruction. Among the sorry 20th century legacy of these age-old campaigns are pogroms, fatwahs and terrorism – not to mention the sectarian hatred that can lead a Greek Orthodox Serb to slay a Bosnian Muslim, an Ulster Protestant to blow up a Catholic Republican, or a Sudanese Muslim to hack to pieces a Sudanese Christian, with all the relish of a pagan joining in a Bacchanalian revel.

If the anthem of the anointed proves all too often to be 'us against them' rather than 'love thy neighbour', religious differences do not always lead to bloodbaths. Sometimes, they simply sow misery.

Witness the hurt inflicted upon one another by Anglicans divided over the issue of women priests. The 11 November 1992 vote by the General Synod of the Church of England brought the traditionalists and the progressives to the barricades, where they pelted one another with insults ('witches', 'misogynists' and much worse) and threats (conversion to Rome). In the storming of the Church of England Bastille, the profound theological divisions over what sort of Christian Anglicans want to be – Protestant? Catholic? – have been buried under the rubble of social, political and sexual accusations and innuendos. Bitter personal antagonisms, which had lain dormant in the hitherto somnolent establishment church of village fetes and Barbara Pym vicars, reared their ugly heads as High Churchers and Low Churchers cast off all thought of the virtues (remember charity, prudence and justice?) and turned their back on key gospel admonishments ('turn the other cheek', 'do unto others...'). Has the feud shown any sign of abating over the past four years? Not one bit: the Church of England risks being turned into a battlefield strewn with discarded dog-collars and dogmas. All in the name of truth, of course.

In the Church of Rome, the liberal versus traditionalist fault line concentrates in an area known as 'reordering'. Shock waves have been sent to the very foundations of the Catholic Church by this campaign, waged by overly-enthusiastic clerics seeking nothing short of changing the architecture of churches up and down the country. Drawing their inspiration – and justification – from the landmark church council of the 1960s, Vatican II, the supporters of reordering argue that all churches must be designed – or redesigned – to reflect the council's new emphasis on the role of the laity. In order to level the difference between clergy and laity (and thereby, in psycho-jargon, to 'empower' the man and woman in the pew), the new-style ecclesiastical architect throws out the baldacchino, pulls out the altar rails, bans the smells and bells, and bulldozes over the desires of mantilla-clad old ladies who draw solace from the way things were. To the non-practising, reordering, in these days of falling church attendance, may seem like the proverbial rearranging of the deckchairs on the Titanic; but to those who seek comfort in a rich liturgical tradition and find confirmation of their faith in the unchanging rites and rituals of the church of their forefathers, the winds of change that now rattle the stained-glass windows have exposed them to a cold climate indeed.

The dark shadow of inner strife also looms over the Evangelicals – the apostles of in-your-face Christianity. Capable of gut-busting professions of faith, marathon public confessions *à la* Oprah Winfrey and irrepressible enthusiasm *à la* Ruby Wax, Evangelical preachers are packing them in from bible-belt America to strait-laced Surrey, from Lima to Liverpool. Amidst shaking tambourines and chanting hallelujahs, the Evangelicals proclaim that the Bible is literally true – and no allowances should be made for the fact that our society is ever so slightly different from the Rome-occupied Judaea where Our Lord lived. With their swelling congregations – drawn from the ranks of Catholic and Anglican faithful – and their bulging coffers, the Evangelicals could well afford to turn a deaf ear to such taunts and slighting epithets as 'happy clappys' from their more prim and proper brothers-and-sisters-in-Christ.

But the group can no longer afford to be smug: threatening its unity is a transatlantic phenomenon known as the 'Toronto Blessing'. Every self-respecting Evangelical indulges in wild-eyed sessions of speaking-in-tongues and rolling in the aisles. But the followers of the Toronto Blessing (launched in a Canadian airport church) have thrown all caution to the wind to exhibit such extreme manifestations of the Holy Spirit as barking like dogs and roaring like lions. Such unorthodox exhibitionism, which has already transformed a number of churches into covered farmyards, would merely raise an ecclesiastical eyebrow, were it not accompanied by blood-chilling apocalyptic visions of an imminent doomsday, fanatical proselytising and exorcisms. But, for the Evangelicals, the sin of all sins lies in the popularity enjoyed by the Toronto Blessing: groupies abound, perhaps drawn by the millenarian prophecies, perhaps by the rowdy farmyard sessions. Whatever the root of its appeal, the rest of the Evangelical community is bent on stamping out the fruits of the Toronto Blessing – and a feud is born.

Before such bitter bickerings, Dean Swift would be right to shake his head and muse upon the little progress Christians have made since the Roundheads and the Cavaliers. But rivalry and disunity are not the exclusive preserve of New Testament followers – a recent row threatens British Jewry as well.

How orthodox should the Orthodox Jew be? How inclusive is United Synagogue Orthodoxy when its women congregants continue to find their every attempt at participation in the community frustrated? Isn't it time that the Orthodox community recognise that some of the greatest achievements this century were being made by secular, as opposed to religious, Jews? Shouldn't the chief rabbi come down from his ivory tower? These were the questions fired at Dr Jonathan Sacks, the chief rabbi, in a virulent attack upon his five-year stewardship published as a letter in *The Jewish Chronicle* in February 1996. When a leading light of the Jewish community – Sir Stanley Kalms, head of Dixon's, no less – calls for the chief rabbi's resignation, the lid is exploded from a Pandora's box of age-old grudges and unsettled disputes. Though his supporters immediately penned a flurry of letters in the rabbi's defence, a Rubicon had been crossed – for when an eminent, humane intellect such as Dr Sacks cannot achieve and maintain unity from within, what hope is there for Britain's religious Jews to withstand the relentless assaults from without?

A sorry spectacle, then, would greet Swift's sailor, shipwrecked upon this isle. For, if the soul is another country, the battle for its dominion – waged by the footsoldiers of secularism against the troops of religion – threatens tò end, in this, the Year of Our Lord 1996, in the disastrous defeat of the battalions of believers. Rent by factionalism, bled dry by petty squabbles and internal bickerings, the faithful conduct themselves as if life were an offensive directed against other belief systems, when they should be rebelling against the stranglehold of modern moral illiteracy.

Our pluralist society, which prides itself on accommodating all ideals and all ways of life, would hasten to dismiss these religious differences as no more than a cautionary tale. But the truth, alas, is much more dangerous: by being riddled with internal conflict, modern-day religions all too often fail to defend us from the barbarians at the gates – those pundits in polo-necks who argue that ethical questions are unsettleable, that moral judgements are taboo and that your evil can be my good. As they trash our teleological heritage, denying that the world has any purpose; as they set fire to our legacy of Judeo-Christian morality; as they throw out of the window the categorical imperative and dance on the graves of our saints and prophets – the barbarians know their attack will not be rebuffed. The believers are busy destroying one another.

CRISTINA ODONE is the editor of *THE CATHOLIC HERALD*. She has recently published her first novel, *THE SHRINE*.

EXTRACT: GULLIVER CAPTURES THE ENEMY FLEET

Another celebrated scene, in which Gulliver saves Lilliput from ATTACK *by seizing the Blefuscan fleet. But his heroic deed gives rise to* JEALOUSIES *which soon mean he has to make his escape back to England.*

I WALKED towards the north-east coast over against Blefuscu; and lying down behind a hillock, took out my small pocket perspective-glass, and viewed the enemy's fleet at anchor, consisting of about fifty men of war, and a great number of transports: I then came back to my house, and gave orders (for which I had a warrant) for a great quantity of the strongest cable and bars of iron. The cable was about as thick as packthread, and the bars of the length and size of a knitting-needle. I trebled the cable to make it stronger, and for the same reason I twisted three of the iron bars together, binding the extremities into a hook. Having thus fixed fifty hooks to as many cables, I went back to the north-east coast, and putting off my coat, shoes, and stockings, walked into the sea in my leathern jerkin, about half an hour before high water. I waded with what haste I could, and swam in the middle about thirty yards till I felt ground; I arrived at the fleet in less than half an hour. The enemy was so frighted when they saw me, that they leaped out of their ships, and swam to shore, where there could not be fewer than thirty thousand souls. I then took my tackling, and fastening a hook to the hole at the prow of each, I tied all the cords together at the end. While I was thus employed, the enemy discharged several thousand arrows, many of which stuck in my hands and face; and besides the excessive smart, gave me much disturbance in my work. My greatest apprehension was for my eyes, which I should have infallibly lost, if I had not suddenly thought of an expedient. I kept among other little necessaries a pair of spectacles in a private pocket, which, as I observed before, had scaped the Emperor's searchers. These I took out and fastened as strongly as I could upon my nose, and thus armed went on boldly with my work in spite of the enemy's arrows, many of which struck against the glasses of my spectacles, but without any other effect, further than a little to discompose them. I had now fastened all the hooks, and taking the knot in my hand, began to pull; but not a ship would stir, for they were all too fast held by their anchors, so that the boldest part of my enterprise remained. I therefore let go the cord, and leaving the hooks fixed to the ships, I resolutely cut with my knife the cables that fastened the anchors, receiving above two hundred shots in my face and hands; then I took up the knotted end of the cables to which my hooks were tied, and with great ease drew fifty of the enemy's largest men-of-war after me.

The Blefuscudians, who had not the least imagination of what I intended, were at first confounded with astonishment. They had seen me cut the cables, and thought my design was only to let the ships run a-drift, or fall foul on each other: but when they perceived the whole fleet moving in order, and saw me pulling at the end, they set up such a scream of grief and despair, that it is almost impossible to describe or conceive. When I had got out of danger, I stopt awhile to pick out the arrows that stuck in my hands and face, and rubbed on some of the same ointment that was given me at my first arrival, as I have formerly mentioned. I then took off my spectacles, and waiting about an hour, till the tide was a little fallen, I waded through the middle with my cargo, and arrived safe at the royal port of Lilliput.

The Emperor and his whole court stood on the shore expecting the issue of this great adventure. They saw the ships move forward in a large half-moon, but could not discern me, who was up to my breast in water. When I advanced to the middle of the channel, they were yet in more pain, because I was under water to my neck. The Emperor concluded me to be drowned, and that the enemy's fleet was approaching in a hostile manner: but he was soon eased of his fears, for the channel growing shallower every step I made, I came in a short time within hearing, and holding up the end of the cable by which the fleet was fastened, I cried in a loud voice, *Long live the most puissant Emperor of Lilliput!*

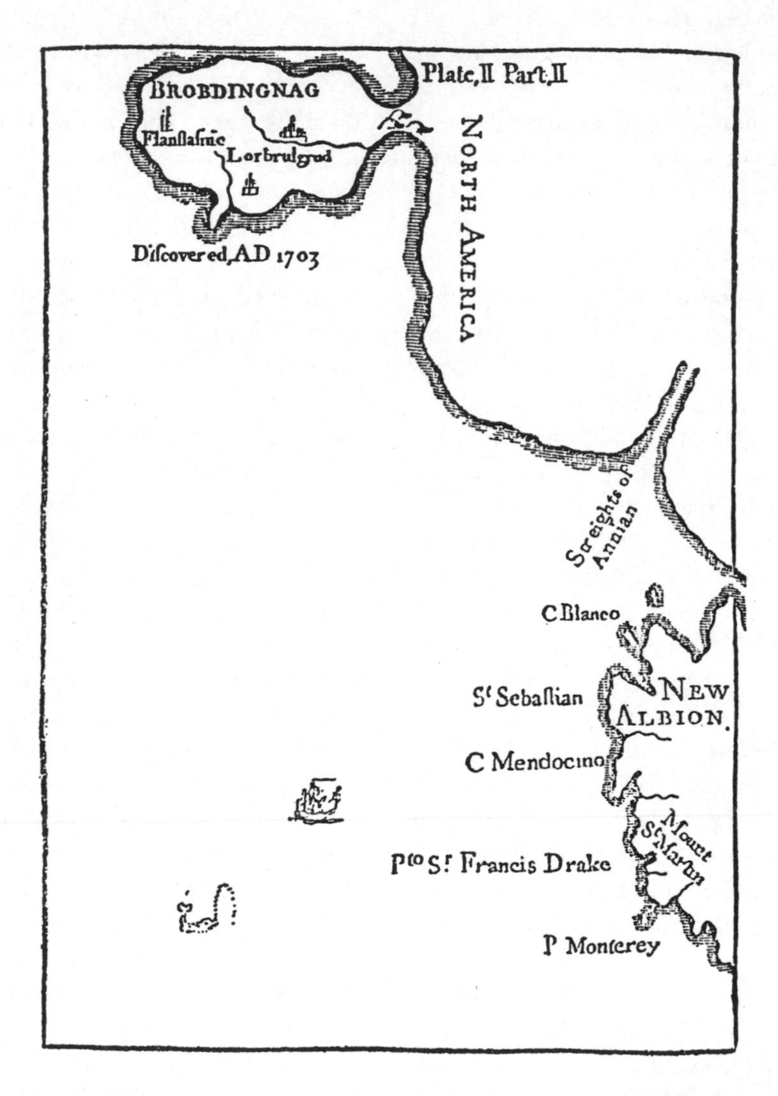

Gulliver's second voyage takes him to Brobdingnag, whose inhabitants are giants. Swift's map shows it as a peninsula jutting out into the Pacific from the North American coast, in the approximate position of Vancouver Island. This coast-line remained uncharted till 1778, as part of the final expedition by Captain James Cook. The great explorer was murdered, in Hawaii, before he could return to England.

EXTRACT: GULLIVER FIGHTS FOR HIS LIFE

The creatures in BROBDINGNAG also come in giant sizes. Gulliver has to fight off a cat, two rats and a monkey – and here gadflies and wasps. ('Glumdalclitch' is his nurse.)

I WAS FREQUENTLY rallied by the Queen upon account of my fearfulness, and she used to ask me whether the people of my country were as great cowards as myself. The occasion was this. The kingdom is much pestered with flies in summer; and these odious insects, each of them as big as a Dunstable lark, hardly gave me any rest while I sat at dinner, with their continual humming and buzzing about my ears. They would sometimes alight upon my victuals; and leave their loathsome excrement or spawn behind, which to me was very visible, though not to the natives of that country, whose large optics were not so acute as mine in viewing smaller objects. Sometimes they would fix upon my nose or forehead, where they stung me to the quick, smelling very offensively, and I could easily trace that viscous matter, which our naturalists tell us enables those creatures to walk with their feet upwards upon a ceiling. I had much ado to defend myself against these detestable animals, and could not forbear starting when they came on my face. It was the common practice of the dwarf to catch a number of these insects in his hand, as schoolboys do among us, and let them out suddenly under my nose, on purpose to frighten me, and divert the Queen. My remedy was to cut them in pieces with my knife as they flew in the air, wherein my dexterity was much admired.

I remember one morning when Glumdalclitch had set me in my box upon a window, as she usually did in fair days to give me air (for I durst not venture to let the box be hung on a nail out of the window, as we do with cages in England) after I had lifted up one of my sashes, and sat down at my table to eat a piece of

sweet cake for my breakfast, above twenty wasps, allured by the smell, came flying into the room, humming louder than the drones of as many bagpipes. Some of them seized my cake, and carried it piecemeal away, others flew about my head and face, confounding me with the noise, and putting me in the utmost terror of their stings. However I had the courage to rise and draw my hanger, and attack them in the air. I dispatched four of them, but the rest got away, and I presently shut my window. These insects were as large as partridges: I took out their stings, found them an inch and a half long, and as sharp as needles.

Gulliver versus the wasps. (Hulton Deutsch)

A gentle, romantic Gulliver. He lies on the ground to kiss the hand of the Emperor of Lilliput.

Painting by R G Mossa, from Hodder & Stoughton's Golden Series of Colour Books *(Hulton Deutsch).*

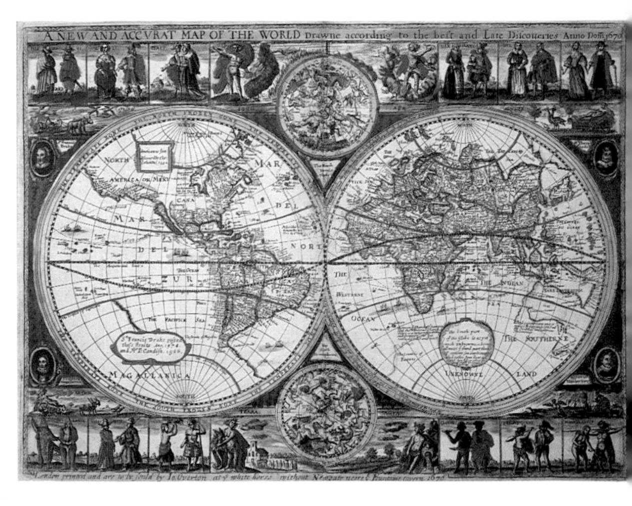
A NEW AND ACCVRAT MAP OF THE WORLD Drawne according to the best and Late Discoueries Anno Dom 1670
NORTH
AMERICA
MAR
DEL
NORT
DEL
ZUR
THE PACIFICK SEA
MAGALLANICA
THE
WESTERNE
OCEAN
THE SOUTHERNE
UNKNOWNE
LAND

Gulliver in Royal Service:
(top left) *capturing the Blefuscu fleet for the Emperor of Lilliput, in the Fleischer Brothers' 1939 cartoon film* (BFI);
(bottom left) *acting as a triumphal arch for a march-past in front of the Emperor, by Gavarni, 1862* (Mary Evans Picture Library);
(top right) *kissing a court lady's hand in Brobdingnag, by the great illustrator of children's books, Arthur Rackham* (Bridgeman Art Library).
Bottom centre: *One version of the world Gulliver set sail in. A map of 1670, partly charted, partly fabulous* (Mary Evans Picture Library).
Bottom right: *The reality behind the fable. The Protestant William III defeats the Catholic James II at the Battle of the Boyne, 1690* (Mary Evans Picture Library).

Is big best? Gulliver (far left) is almost eaten as a titbit by a Brobdingnagian infant, in a mid-19th century illustration (Mary Evans Picture Library); (bottom) he is exhibited to a Brobdingnag farmer, in a painting by the Victorian artist, Richard Redgrave (Bridgeman Art Library); while (left) William and Mary accept the English crown, in a late 17th century engraving, against a background of humble and diminutive subjects (Mary Evans Picture Library).

Above: *The power broker. Sir Robert Walpole, corrupt but effective, became Britain's first-ever Prime Minister (in office 1721-42). As a Whig, he finally buried any prospect of the Tory Swift's advancement* (Bridgeman Art Library).
Opposite: *Mad, and not so mad, scientists. Gulliver* (bottom) *catches sight of Laputa, kept airborne by its ingenious inventions, in an illustration by Grandville. Once aloft* (top left), *he can consult the island's bizarre, mathematics-mad King* (Mary Evans Picture Library). *Sir Isaac Newton, now revered, is the kind of thinker Swift deeply mistrusted; he might have enjoyed this picture* (top right), *from a Swedish family magazine of the 1920s, showing Newton solemnly blowing bubbles in order to study gravity* (Mary Evans Picture Library).

Above: On the outside looking in. Gulliver (played by Ted Danson, in the 1996 Jim Henson Productions Film) keeps an eye on the courtiers of Lilliput.

The fruits of victory. The Duke of Marlborough wins the battle of Blenheim, on the Danube, 1704 (left)*. This thwarted the French (Catholic) King Louis XIV's ambition to dominate Europe* (Mary Evans Picture Library)*. The allegorical painting* (above) *hangs in Blenheim Palace, Oxfordshire, which was given to the Marlborough/Churchill family by a grateful nation. Queen Anne presents the architectural plans of the palace to a figure who symbolises military merit* (Mary Evans Picture Library).

ANSWERS

eorge I (left) was brought over from Hanover in 1714 to ensure the rotestant succession. He never learned to speak English and was eeply unpopular. The awkward, guttural languages that Swift vents for the peoples Gulliver visits may be a parody of George's ative German (Bridgeman Art Library).
the scientific academy of Laputa, they claim to have the answer to l life's problems. But as Gulliver finds (below left, in the 1996 Jim Henson oductions Film) they don't. The only answer is to copy the kindly, tional Houyhnhnms and strive to distance oneself from the brutal, l too human Yahoos. Below: Gulliver's Houyhnhnm master rebukes m, in a painting by the 18th century artist Sawrey Gilpin, for aising the glories of war (Bridgeman Art Library). Right: The horses reverse e wrongs done to them in Europe and put the Yahoos to ll the plough (Milo Winter).

Water, water, everywhere: Gulliver (Ted Danson) sails away on his raft.

Extract: The King of Brobdingnag Passes Judgement

Gulliver has been explaining to the King of Brobdingnag how English SOCIETY *is organised. The King listens carefully, and then passes judgment. ('Grildrig' is the name Gulliver is known by among the Brobdingnagians.)*

My little friend Grildrig, you have made a most admirable panegyric upon your country; you have clearly proved that ignorance, idleness, and vice, may be sometimes the only ingredients for qualifying a legislator; that laws are best explained, interpreted, and applied by those whose interest and abilities lie in perverting, confounding, and eluding them. I observe among you some lines of an institution, which in its original might have been tolerable, but these half erased, and the rest wholly blurred and blotted by corruptions. It doth not appear from all you have said, how any one virtue is required towards the procurement of any one station among you; much less that men are ennobled on account of their virtue, that priests are advanced for their piety or learning, soldiers for their conduct or valour, judges for their integrity, senators for the love of their country, or counsellors for their wisdom. As for yourself (continued the King) who have spent the greatest part of your life in travelling, I am well disposed to hope you may hitherto have escaped many vices of your country. But by what I have gathered from your own relation, and the answers I have with much pains wringed and extorted from you, I cannot but conclude the bulk of your natives to be the most pernicious race of little odious vermin that nature ever suffered to crawl upon the surface of the earth.

EXTRACT: TWO EARS OF CORN

The King tells Gulliver his simple RULES *for governing a country well. They include making sure that people don't die of famine. As so often in the book, there is a clear analogy with the way England* RULED *Ireland.*

I REMEMBER very well, in a discourse one day with the King, when I happened to say there were several thousand books among us written upon the art of government, it gave him (directly contrary to my intention) a very mean opinion of our understandings. He professed both to abominate and despise all mystery, refinement, and intrigue, either in a prince or a minister. He could not tell what I meant by secrets of state, where an enemy or some rival nation were not in the case. He confined the knowledge of governing within very narrow bounds; to common sense and reason, to justice and lenity, to the speedy determination of civil and criminal causes; with some other obvious topics, which are not worth considering. And he gave it for his opinion, that whoever could make two ears of corn or two blades of grass to grow upon a spot of ground where only one grew before, would deserve better of mankind, and do more essential service to his country than the whole race of politicians put together.

Gulliver with the King of Brobdingnag, by French caricaturist Gavarni, 1862.
(Mary Evans Picture Library)

TOO MANY EARS OF CORN

GEORGE MONBIOT *argues that an obsession with productivity has ruined the land*

ONLY an ungrateful nation could forget the debt we owe to the King of Brobdingnag and his timely suggestions about growing two ears of corn where one grew before. Had he not been so kind as to remind us of our obligations to the needy, we might never have engaged upon a project which must surely rank among our most enduring sources of pride. Indeed, so diligent has been Britain's discharge of these duties that it now spends more money on this enterprise than it could ever hope to recoup.

Malicious tongues among us have suggested that credit for this accomplishment should rest wholly with the good offices of the European Union and its Common Agricultural Policy. Nothing could be further from the truth. We have achieved this breakthrough only by means of centuries of patriotic endeavour and national sacrifice. For, as our historians have now established, upon returning to England Mr Gulliver wasted no time in promulgating the monarch's wise words. Scarcely had he set foot once more on his native soil than politicians of all persuasions began to abandon the self-interested pursuit of wealth and power and devote themselves to the welfare of the people.

From approximately 1730 onwards, members of parliament started to display a robust interest in agricultural improvement. Neglecting the less pressing affairs of state, they passed, over the next 120 years, no fewer than 4,200 Acts of Enclosure. The Acts empowered special commissioners to divide up and enclose with hedges the commons which had provided for the wasteful subsistence of England's innumerable cottars, copyholders and small freeholders. They had the effect of sensibly dispensing with the customary rights that were such an impediment to progress, and placing absolute control of the land in the hands of certain individuals, freeing them to engage in agricultural improvements of the kind the King of Brobdingnag had envisaged.

By a happy and wholly unanticipated coincidence, most of the beneficiaries of these reforms were large landowners. As most members of parliament happened to be substantial proprietors themselves, their disinterested work on behalf of the poor was, by good fortune, rewarded. Sir Thomas Coke, of Holkham in Norfolk, was one of the landlords who first put his new powers to the service of the nation. Between 1778 and 1794, he raised the value of his land from £5,000 a year to £20,000 a year by means of new agricultural techniques. His patriotic example was swiftly followed by other enlightened proprietors and grain, sheep and cattle production were all enormously enhanced in order to furnish the exchequer and feed the hungry.

It was, of course, true that some trifling number of the rural poor – a few hundred thousand at most – lost, in the course of the enclosures, the ability to feed themselves. But this petty inconvenience was more than offset by the unrivalled opportunities with which they were now presented. Many were, for example, able to enjoy the redeeming virtues of hard work provided by the landlords. Others were able to move to the cities, where they could render service to their country by labouring, in conditions of noble self-sacrifice, for up to 18 hours a day in the factories, while receiving a wage which barely ensured their survival.

For reasons best known to themselves, however, the dispossessed commoners failed to demonstrate the full measure of their gratitude for these new opportunities. Far from thanking their benefactors, they rioted repeatedly, setting fire to hayricks, damaging the landlords' houses and destroying the new hedges. Fortunately, justices of the peace were conveniently placed to deal with this insurrection, for most of them were landowners. With the help of the yeomanry, they brought the full impartiality of the law to bear on these impertinent wretches – hundreds were hanged, transported or imprisoned for life. Our representatives' concern for the moral welfare of the people was such that they begrudged no amount of patient effort in dealing with even the most inconsequential of these matters. The new capital offences they introduced allowed rogues who broke windows, pulled down fences or knocked landlords' hats off their heads to be hanged for their insolence.

Perhaps the agricultural labourers, who remained so strangely ungrateful for the new prosperity introduced to the countryside, failed to understand that the high price the landowners continued to receive for their grain was good for the agricultural economy, as indeed was the reduction of the workers' negligible wages. Indeed, thousands of those who starved to death utterly failed to comprehend how beneficial these arrangements were.

To ensure that they persisted, the representatives who had forgone the selfish pursuit of petty politics in deference to the King of Brobdingnag's wishes, passed, from 1815 onwards, a new series of far-sighted Acts. The Corn Laws ensured that landowners would always find a good price for their grain, as they forbade the importation of foreign wheat until domestic prices had fallen below a certain level – in other words, grain could only be imported when it was least needed. Having thus secured the viability of the agricultural sector, our reformed politicians then concentrated on stimulating the economy still further by selflessly squandering their money. While the peasants starved for want of enterprise, the landlords sought to demonstrate to them what the fruits of hard labour could deliver, by means of balls and banquets, fine clothes and follies, brandy, hunting and whoring.

When the prime minister, Sir Robert Peel, so short-sightedly sought to restrain the enterprise economy by repealing the Corn Laws, the honourable members demonstrated their disgust at this blatant attempt to mix politics with the imperative of food production, by opposing him as best as they were able. At length, however, his revolutionary tendencies, so cunningly concealed earlier in his career, prevailed. But to ensure that politics and food production remained wholly separate affairs, agricultural labourers were denied the vote until 1884.

Over the next one hundred years, land holding in Britain was gradually rationalised. Today, with one of the highest concentrations of ownership in the world, our landlords are a source of enduring pride to the nation. Their approach to agriculture combines the best of modern technology and traditional values. Sensibly, they have no truck with such ephemeral conceits as democratic accountability, landscape protection or market mechanisms, but plough on irrespective of such fads. Our politicians, meanwhile, have remained patriotically committed to sustaining the triumphant pace of agricultural improvement.

After the Second World War, the British government decided that our vulnerable nation should never again be dependent on imports of basic foods for its sustenance. So, to free us from the necessity of buying foreign grain, it subsidised the purchase of machinery, pesticides and fertiliser, and the resulting transformation of the industry. Fortunately for international trade, nearly all of our tractors and chemicals are imported from abroad. Though we would swiftly starve in the unfortunate event of war, the degree of technological innovation on our farms should be a source of admiration. Britain is now such an advanced nation that it employs fewer people in farming as a proportion of the population than does the city state of Hong Kong.

In introducing these changes, we have dispensed with many cumbersome and unnecessary obstacles, not the least of which is soil. For centuries, farmers laboured under the misapprehension that they needed soil in order to grow crops. Thanks to the felicitous introduction of deep ploughing, and the accompanying relocation of much of this vexatious dirt into the sea, we are able to demonstrate that such antediluvian practices need have no place in modern agriculture. Crops can be grown on little more than shingle, with sufficient applications of fertiliser.

We have disposed, too, of many of the unsightly lumps and ridges which once disfigured our agricultural landscape. The barrows, hill forts, field systems and ancient lanes which mired us in the past and intruded on our views of the wholesome earth, have already been erased from many parts of Britain, and farmers are seeking to complete the task as rapidly as possible. Modern agriculture has successfully eliminated such irritations as skylarks, song-thrushes and nightingales from many parts of their ranges, immersing the countryside in a deep and lasting peace. It has relieved us of the burden of insect life, and the distraction of wild flowers.

But no measure of success in modern agriculture is as uplifting as the tremendous boost to food production these new techniques have precipitated. Indeed, so well stocked are our granaries that hundreds of millions are spent each year in storing and destroying surplus food. In raising output so markedly, we not only maintain our landowners in the noble style to which they are accustomed, but also guarantee our pre-eminence in the global marketplace, by averting the possibility of self-reliance in the developing world.

In Britain, such foresight costs the taxpayer a mere £2 billion a year – a competitive price for such selfless service to humankind. Yet we refuse to rest on our laurels. So determined are we to grow three, four, even 10 ears of corn or its equivalent where but one grew before, that we are now trying to introduce parts of bacteria into plants, scorpions into caterpillars and humans into pigs. As humble citizens of a trifling land, our only regret must surely be that the King of Brobdingnag cannot be present to marvel at how assiduously we have followed his advice.

GEORGE MONBIOT writes a *GUARDIAN* column on the environment. He founded the *LAND IS OURS* campaign and is a Newbury by-pass protester. His books include *AMAZON WATERSHED*.

EXTRACT: GULLIVER AS A PLAYTHING FOR THE COURT LADIES

At the royal court in Brobdingnag, Gulliver finds he is regarded as a TOY – a person of 'no sort of consequence'. Swift here uses the device of magnification to express his DISGUST at human vanity, just as he had earlier used the trick of miniaturisation.

THAT WHICH gave me most uneasiness among these Maids of Honour, when my nurse carried me to visit them, was to see them use me without any manner of ceremony, like a creature who had no sort of consequence. For they would strip themselves to the skin, and put on their smocks in my presence, while I was placed on their toilet directly before their naked bodies, which, I am sure, to me was very far from being a tempting sight, or from giving me any other emotions than those of horror and disgust. Their skins appeared so coarse and uneven, so variously coloured, when I saw them near, with a mole here and there as broad as a trencher, and hairs hanging from it thicker than pack-threads, to say nothing further concerning the rest of their persons. Neither did they at all scruple, while I was by, to discharge what they had drunk, to the quantity of at least two hogsheads, in a vessel that held above three tuns. The handsomest among these Maids of Honour, a pleasant frolicsome girl of sixteen, would sometimes set me astride upon one of her nipples, with many other tricks, wherein the reader will excuse me for not being over particular. But I was so much displeased, that I entreated Glumdalclitch to contrive some excuse for not seeing that young lady any more.

Gulliver with Brobdingnag court ladies. (Mary Evans Picture Library)

Gulliver's third voyage takes him to the airborne island of Laputa and other near-by lands. Laputa floats, by magnetic power, above its island colony of Balnibarbi. The Laputans are obsessed by every kind of science. The neighbouring island of Luggnagg is chiefly notable for the 'Struldbrugs', a group of people who live for ever. On Swift's map, these islands, not far from Japan, don't correspond to any existing territories; this area of the Pacific is empty of land. The Kuril Islands are the closest equivalent. Swift would have been delighted by the fact that sovereignty over them has been constantly disputed between Japan and Russia.

EXTRACT: THE END OF LAPUTA IS EVER NIGH

The inhabitants of the flying island of Laputa have ABANDONED common sense in their exaggerated reverence for scientific research. They are in a CONSTANT state of panic over the scientists' latest scare story.

THESE PEOPLE are under continual disquietudes, never enjoying a minute's peace of mind; and their disturbances proceed from causes which very little affect the rest of mortals. Their apprehensions arise from several changes they dread in the celestial bodies. For instance that the earth, by the continual approaches of the sun towards it, must in course of time be absorbed or swallowed up. That the face of the sun will by degrees be encrusted with its own effluvia, and give no more light to the world. That the earth very narrowly escaped a brush from the tail of the last comet, which would have infallibly reduced it to ashes; and that the next, which they have calculated for one and thirty years hence, will probably destroy us. For if in its perihelion it should approach within a certain degree of the sun (as by their calculations they have reason to dread) it will conceive a degree of heat ten thousand times more intense than that of red-hot glowing iron; and in its absence from the sun, carry a blazing tail ten hundred thousand and fourteen miles long; through which if the earth should pass at the distance of one hundred thousand miles from the nucleus or main body of the comet, it must in its passage be set on fire, and reduced to ashes. That the sun daily spending its rays without any nutriment to supply them, will at last be wholly consumed and annihilated; which must be attended with the destruction of this earth, and of all the planets that receive their light from it.

They are so perpetually alarmed with the apprehensions of these and the like impending dangers, that they can neither sleep quietly in their beds, nor have any relish for the common pleasures or amusements of life. When they meet an acquaintance in the morning, the first question is about the sun's health, how he looked at his setting and rising, and what hopes they have to avoid the stroke of the approaching comet. This conversation they are apt to run into with the same temper that boys discover, in delighting to hear terrible stories of sprites and hobgoblins, which they greedily listen to, and dare not go to bed for fear.

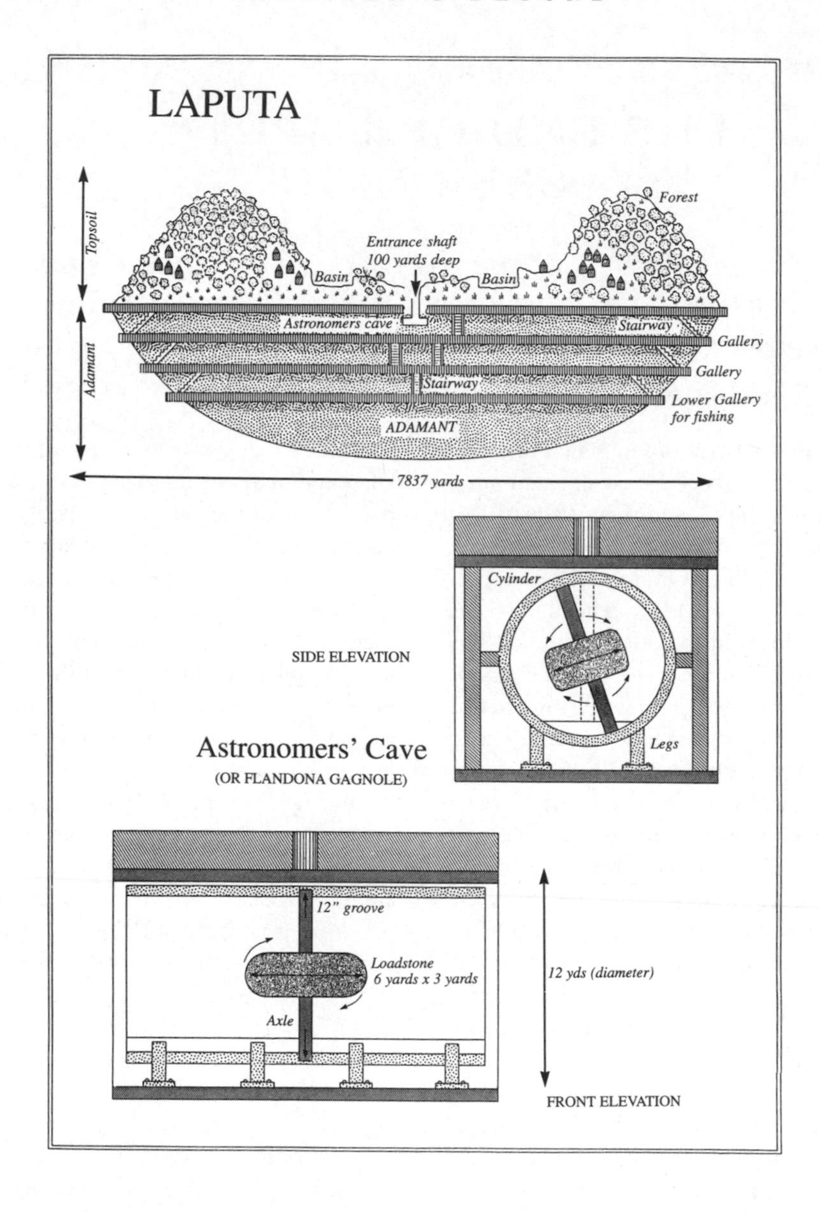

A 20th century interpretation of the inner workings of Laputa. A revolving magnet (or loadstone) keeps the island aloft by attraction and repulsion. It is fixed in a cave inside Laputa's supporting base of 'adamant', a fabulously hard rock.

(From The Dictionary of Imaginary Places, *Granada Publishing, 1980. © Graham Greenfield, by permission of David Bolt Associates)*

MILES KINGTON *wonders why we are such suckers for scientific and medical research*

THERE is a general impression that things in the 20th century have gradually got better and better, but a moment's thought will show that this is not so. The 20th century began with the invention of *Reader's Digest* and ended with the supremacy of the sound bite. In other words, it went downhill.

At the time, people thought that the *Reader's Digest* represented defeat, because it meant that people could master nothing longer than summaries. That looks very impressive in retrospect, as now we can think only in terms of headlines. As we become more and more educated and informed, our comprehension becomes smaller and smaller. A hundred years ago people were talking about quite complicated issues such as 'The Irish Question' and 'The Bulgarian Question' and 'The Balkan Question'. Nowadays we cannot manage anything much more sophisticated than being for or against Europe, which is of course meaningless.

It is a pity, really. This century was going to be such a sensible century, so rational, so scientific, so full of planning. Even now, with only a few years to go to its end, we are being told that information is the key to everything, that information technology will get us there, that IT is the path.

(Funny how the meaning of 'It' changes. Once, in the 1920s, it was sex appeal. 'The girl with It'. In my father's day it was Italian vermouth – 'gin and It'. Now IT is raiding databases. All three have proved fallible, one after the other.)

To put it another way, the more we know, we more we are afraid of. It wasn't meant to be this way. It should be the other way round. We should get increasing confidence with increasing knowledge, but what actually happens is that the more we know, the more bogies in the dark we see.

Here is a brief list of things we are scared of at this moment.

Global warming.
The hole in the ozone layer.
AIDS.
Not winning the lottery.
The seas being fished out.
The rain forests being cut down.
Drugs.
Being killed by cancer or a serial killer or
a police car on its way to help someone.
Rupert Murdoch.
Things from outer space
The Bermuda Triangle...

Of all these, I think the Bermuda Triangle is the most interesting because we still believe in its dangers, although it has often been proved that almost all the maritime accidents which take place in it have rational explanations. There was a book on the Bermuda Triangle's mysteries which sold very well. There was another one explaining the mysteries which did not sell very well. And this is because people did not want the Bermuda Triangle, and its disappearing ships, explained. They like to be frightened. They *like* to be mystified, even if the mystery might kill them.

One example of this is the way we manufacture a new scare when an old scare is cleared up.

When doctors had tamed the good old sexually transmitted diseases such as gonorrhoea and syphilis which had scared everyone since goodness knows when, herpes came along to fill the gap, but it was only a holding operation till AIDS arrived.

When the fear of nuclear holocaust ebbed away with the end of the Cold War, we didn't relax; we immediately got scared by the thought of nuclear arms falling into the hands of smaller countries, perhaps Islamic countries, perhaps worst of all into the hands of terrorists.

When the fear of nuclear war died away, it didn't remove the fear of nuclear peace, as exemplified by Chernobyl. We find it terribly quaint that Shakespeare's yokels should predict disaster because of the births of two-headed calves and five-legged sheep, yet our comedians say exactly the same thing about the country round Sellafield, even though none of them has ever seen a two-headed anything, or indeed been to Sellafield.

The ultimate scare-person in today's eyes would be a figure which was thought at first to be an alien from outer space and then turned out merely to be an Islamic fundamentalist terrorist armed with nuclear weapons rushing towards us waving an HIV-infected syringe.

And, of course, smoking.

Passive smoking was a new invention of the 1980s, an ingenious extension of danger whereby you could be at risk from someone *else* in your neighbourhood doing something risky, almost as if suicide turned out to be contagious. Passive drinking and passive sex have not yet been invented, unless you count the accidental passing on of HIV, but passive music has been identified by Pipedown, an organisation dedicated to curtailing canned music, and passive driving, or being killed by cars, has been with us for a long time.

Smoking was once upon a time a harmless hobby which had no drawbacks except the fall of ash. In Victorian days smoking was thought to be no worse than wearing hair cream. The wily Victorians invented things to counter both. The antimacassar to beat hair cream, and the smoking jacket to beat smoking. Alas, we now know that smoking jackets, however decorative, cannot cure cancer. But it does show that the most delicious way in which humans can frighten themselves is to discover that something we take for granted as part of everyday life can actually kill you.

I don't know if hair cream ever became a major health hazard, but I do know that in the 1920s some cigarettes were advertised as being 'kind to your throat', so it wasn't till some time later that smoking became a cause of throat cancer.

In the 1960s fluoride was added to water to strengthen our teeth and shortly afterwards became a major scare.

In the 1980s things accelerated and we became scared of butter, milk, salt, red meat, wine, and almost everything in the home except olive oil and balsamic vinegar.

Even homely things like glue became major threats, because kids discovered you could sniff it and get addicted to it.

In the 1990s we have put beef on the list because of mad cow disease and in the last few weeks, as I write, electricity pylons have been promoted from being part of the landscape to being among the major causes of cancer.

Fear has become part of our culture, not in a manic way but in a pleasant background twitchy sort of way like the ticking of Radio 1 or the fizz of fizzy water or the hum of the computer. (Incidentally, remember the fizzy water death threat when all Perrier was removed from the shelves for a while in case it killed us? That was a good one!)

Fear is part of the way we think. We favour the big bang theory as an explanation for the start of the universe, because we think that's the way it may be going to end as well, and it seems symmetrical to have a big bang at both ends. The 1980s and 1990s became obsessed with dinosaurs. Why? We had known about them for a century or more without getting too interested. So why now? Because dinosaurs ruled the earth and then suddenly got wiped out, that's why, and we rule the earth and we think deep down that we are going to be wiped out too.

Most of these fears are irrational and there is absolutely no point in worrying about any of them. Even the rational fears seem to produce no action on our part. For example, it is proved, time and time again, that various parts of Britain have the worst and fattiest diets in the world (usually Glasgow or Northern Ireland) and that the British diet as a whole is ghastly enough to overload the National Health Service. All people have to do to live well is to eat well and exercise well – that's all – but they refuse to do so, and prefer to wait till they are carted off to hospital to complain about the NHS.

The Americans are wiser than us in this respect. They actually get out and *do* something about their fears. They have various tried and tested methods of dealing with problems. These are as follows.

1 Suing someone for $13,000,000.

2 Having plastic surgery, either to decrease a chin or increase a bust.

3 Sending the troops in to Haiti or Somalia or Bosnia.

These methods have all been tried and tested by the Americans. That doesn't mean they work. In fact, the result of the trying and testing is that we now know that none of them works, but does that discourage the Americans? No! They are too optimistic to let failure get them down or even notice it, which is why they will still be the greatest nation even when Singapore has overtaken their GNP.

In Britain, our solutions to problems are all smaller scale and untried and untested.

1 Winning the national lottery.

2 Reading Hello! *magazine.*

3 Reflecting that however many problems you have got,
at least you are not as badly off as the royal family.

Will it be enough? Frankly, I do not think it will be. And that is why I am a deeply worried person. Very worried. Every time a scientist comes on Melvyn Bragg's *Start The Week* and tells us that if we just stick with science, whether it's chemistry or physics or genetics...

Ah, genetics !

When I discovered that geneticists have now discovered a way of giving our modern tasteless watery tomatoes a longer shelf-life, I knew it was time to despair.

MILES KINGTON is a humorous columnist and jazz player. His many books include *THE FRANGLAIS LIEUTENANT'S WOMAN.*

EXTRACT:

GULLIVER LEARNS OF THE IMMORTAL STRULDBRUGS

On the island of Luggnagg some CHILDREN in each generation, the Struldbrugs, are born with the gift (or curse) of eternal life. They don't have the benefit of eternal youth.

AFTER THIS preface he gave me a particular account of the *struldbrugs* among them. He said they commonly acted like mortals, till about thirty years old, after which by degrees they grew melancholy and dejected, increasing in both till they came to fourscore. This he learned from their own confession; for otherwise there not being above two or three of that species born in an age, they were too few to form a general observation by. When they came to fourscore years, which is reckoned the extremity of living in this country, they had not only all the follies and infirmities of other old men, but many more which arose from the dreadful prospect of never dying. They were not only opinionative, peevish, covetous, morose, vain, talkative, but uncapable of friendship, and dead to all natural affection, which never descended below their grandchildren. Envy and impotent desires are their prevailing passions. But those objects against which their envy seems principally directed, are the vices of the younger sort, and the deaths of the old. By reflecting on the former, they find themselves cut off from all possibility of pleasure; and whenever they see a funeral, they lament and repine that others have gone to a harbour of rest, to which they themselves never can hope to arrive. They have no remembrance of anything but what they learned and observed in their youth and middle age, and even that is very imperfect. And for the truth or particulars of any fact, it is safer to depend on common traditions than upon their best recollections. The least miserable among them appear to be those who turn to dotage, and entirely lose their memories; these meet with more pity and assistance, because they want many bad qualities which abound in others.

If a *struldbrug* happen to marry one of his own kind, the marriage is dissolved of course by the courtesy of the kingdom, as soon as the younger of the two comes to be fourscore. For the law thinks it a reasonable indulgence, that those who are condemned without any fault of their own to a perpetual continuance in the world, should not have their misery doubled by the load of a wife.

As soon as they have completed the term of eighty years, they are looked on as dead in law; their heirs immediately succeed to their estates, only a small pittance is reserved for their support, and the poor ones are maintained at the public charge. After that period they are held incapable of any employment of trust or profit, they cannot purchase lands or take leases, neither are they allowed to be witnesses in any cause, either civil or criminal, not even for the decision of meers and bounds [i.e. boundary disputes].

At ninety they lose their teeth and hair, they have at that age no distinction of taste, but eat and drink whatever they can get, without relish or appetite. The diseases they were subject to still continue without increasing or diminishing. In talking they forget the common appellation of things, and the names of persons, even of those who are their nearest friends and relations. For the same reason they never can amuse themselves with reading, because their memory will not serve to carry them from the beginning of a sentence to the end; and by this defect they are deprived of the only entertainment whereof they might otherwise be capable.

The language of this country being always upon the flux, the *struldbrugs* of one age do not understand those of another, neither are they able after two hundred years to hold any conversation (farther than by a few general words) with their neighbours the mortals; and thus they lie under the disadvantage of living like foreigners in their own country.

This was the account given me of the *struldbrugs*, as near as I can remember. I afterwards saw five or six of different ages, the youngest not above two hundred years old, who were brought to me at several times by some of my friends; but although they were told that I was a great traveller, and had seen all the world, they had not the least curiosity to ask me a question; only desired I would give them a *slumskudask*, or a token of remembrance, which is a modest way of begging, to avoid the law that strictly forbids it, because they are provided for by the public, although indeed with a very scanty allowance.

Hope I Die Before I Get *Old*

POLLY TOYNBEE *finds Swift's vision of a geriatric society uncomfortably prophetic*

I RE-READ with astonishment that extraordinary part of *Gulliver's Travels* where he discovers the Struldbrugs – the immortal ones who cannot die. Astonishment because Swift is so prescient about what might happen if people did live forever – or, as nowadays, survive for decades longer than was usual in his lifetime.

Gulliver is told about the curious Struldbrugs, rare children immediately identified at birth by the red spot on their forehead, denoting that they will never die. He fondly imagines that this must be the cause of great celebration within a family. He starts to conjecture on the qualities of these ancient people. Of the nation he says, 'Happy people who enjoy so many living examples of ancient virtue, and have masters ready to instruct them in the wisdom of all former ages!' How happy must the lucky Struldbrugs themselves be – 'born exempt from that universal calamity of human nature, having their minds free and disengaged, without the weight and depression caused by the continual apprehension of death.'

His hosts listen to him with wry amusement, as he fantasizes gleefully on what he would do were he born a Struldbrug. He would start by amassing a fortune, which by wise investment would grow to astronomical sums over the centuries, making him the richest man in the kingdom eventually. (Swift is right – the greedy galloping pension funds of old age will soon own every business on earth.) He imagines himself learning everything, and recording everything that happens, becoming 'a living treasury of knowledge'.

His hosts disabuse him: they explain that the Struldbrugs have immortality, but not perpetual youth. When they reach 80, 'they had not only all the follies and infirmities of other old men, but many more which arose from the dreadful prospect of never dying. They were not only opinionative, peevish, covetous, morose, vain, talkative, but uncapable of friendship, and dead to all natural affection, which never descended below their grand-children. Envy and impotent desires are their prevailing passions. But those objects against which their envy seems principally directed, are the vices of the younger sort.' There is much more of this. The Struldbrugs have no recollection of anything beyond their youth, so they are useless even as living historical records.

How does the state cope with these beings? At 80 they are regarded 'as dead in law: their heirs immediately succeed to their estates, only a small pittance is reserved for their support' (equivalent to our state pension). Their marriages are dissolved at 80 since it is deemed an unnatural cruelty to expect people to stay married forever. (Modern divorce figures owe much to increased longevity and life expectation.) The laws against the Struldbrugs' ownership of property spring from this idea: 'As avarice is the necessary consequent of old age, those immortals would in time become proprietors of the whole nation, and engross the civil power.'

So should we, too, start to fear the 'grey power' of our rapidly ageing population? At the start of the National Health Service in 1947, the year of my own birth, only one per cent of people lived to a great old age, into their 80s. Very few people lived to receive a telegram from the Queen on their 100th birthday, but now she's sending them out by the bagful. By 1981 the number of over-80s reached nearly three per cent, and will number around six per cent by 2011. When we NHS post-war bulge babies reach retirement, we will indeed prove ourselves to be a monstrous generation. Already, tracking our progress through to our late 40s, we have shifted the culture of the nation in our favour every step of the way. First when we were young we brought power to youth for the first time. Now we are responsible for the Beatles and the Rolling Stones still being the totemic elderly figures they are.

By the time we reach 60, in the year 2007, you can bet we will have new laws on the statute books preventing any form of age discrimination or compulsory retirement. We will want to hold onto our jobs as long as we can, and in doing so, we will be building up even fatter pensions. Swift's avarice of the old will show itself in our disregard for the lack of opportunity offered to the young, as we old guard cling to our posts and our power. However much we fail in imagination and innovation, we will be good at blocking the rise of the puny generations below us, clothing our selfishness piously in the sententious language of 'ageism', as if it were really as pernicious as sexism or racism, which it is not. The ill-fated generations that come after us are doomed to suffer under our economic hegemony and then, as we become frail, to pay out of their wages for our extensive and very expensive care.

Luckily the British are in a better economic position to cope with an ageing population than our main competitors. The burden of the state pension has been reduced virtually to the Struldbrugian 'pittance'. Many more people have good private pensions here than in France, Germany, Japan and Sweden which will all have a much worse worker-to-retiree ratio, and much greater obligations to pay out state pensions. This may turn to our advantage, as their economies falter. They will need to import more goods, as they will not have the workforce to produce enough themselves, even with advanced robotic skills.

As long as governments present and future hold firm in Britain over the essential principle that the better-off old should and must use their capital and savings to pay for their own care, then the burden on the young will be lessened. But John Major has been moved by the angry cries of the middle class old, who claim they paid taxes and National Insurance all their working life and now deserve to have the welfare state pay for their care, from cradle to grave, as promised. Currently when they need residential or nursing care, the state takes whatever money they have beyond £16,000, or sells up their home to cover the cost. Unjust, cry the old! Where is the reward for prudence, a life-time's savings, if they cannot pass it down to their children?

But the principle was enshrined in the 1948 National Assistance Act. It was rarely used, because in those days few old people had any capital. Now that two-thirds of pensioners own their own home, they discover they must pay for what was free for their poorer parents. This wracks the consciences of the Tories, as guardians of the inheritances of middle England, spurred on by vigorous campaigns by the *Daily Express* and *Sunday Times*. But it is essential the principle is maintained. The right of mostly well-off children in their mid-50s, already with paid-off mortgages, to inherit from their parents has to be sacrificed to the needs of a small generation of workers not to be over-burdened with taxes to pay for care of the elderly.

So much for the politics and economics of the modern Struldbrugs. But what of the morality? Gulliver noted that the people among whom the Struldbrugs lived had lost their fear of death, since they could see before their eyes the horror of perpetual life. He wanted to take a couple of Struldbrugs home with him to Britain, so his fellow citizens could also gaze upon their predicament and lose their fear of death too. 'The reader will easily believe, that from what I had heard and seen, my keen appetite for perpetuity of life was much abated ... no tyrant could invent a death into which I would not run with pleasure from such a life.'

We have homes and psycho-geriatric wards I could take you, dear reader, to visit that would fill your heart with fear of too long a life. Nodding, drooling, often wailing rows of Struldbrugs sit and wait for a death that will not come. Their miserable bodies have out-lived their minds. Alzheimer's is becoming an epidemic as people outlive their brains. The tiny shreds of consciousness that remain cause mainly more suffering. They suffer acute paranoid delusions, living in terror of everything they cannot comprehend, recognising nothing and no one as familiar. They should be on public display, as a warning to us all not to outlive our senses.

The Roman Catholics have a prayer to St Joseph for a happy death. Most people surveying these Struldbrugs would pray devoutly that they should not end this way. It is a pretty false moral squeamishness that prevents us from killing them, putting them out of a misery far more intense than some race-horse with a broken leg, or elderly family pet. I have never understood why animals should be afforded this mercy as a kindness, but not humans.

However, we are unlikely to be hard-headed and realistic enough ever to dare frame such a law. But as a matter of urgency, it should be possible for those of us who choose to sign a document demanding death once we are mentally beyond being able to make the request for ourselves. It is not enough to ask for no treatment, hoping that pneumonia, the old man's friend, will do the business. Many live on for years without the need for medication. Swift's message is that Struldbrugs suffer and cause suffering all around them, and he would rightly have put them out of their misery if he could.

POLLY TOYNBEE is an associate editor of *THE INDEPENDENT* and a writer and broadcaster on social issues.

GULLIVERS TRAVELS,
forming part of
Cooke's Pocket Edition of
SELECT NOVELS
or Novelist's Entertaining Library
containing a Complete Collection of
Universally Approved
Adventures Tales &c by the most Esteem'd Authors.
Superbly Embellished

(Mary Evans Picture Library)

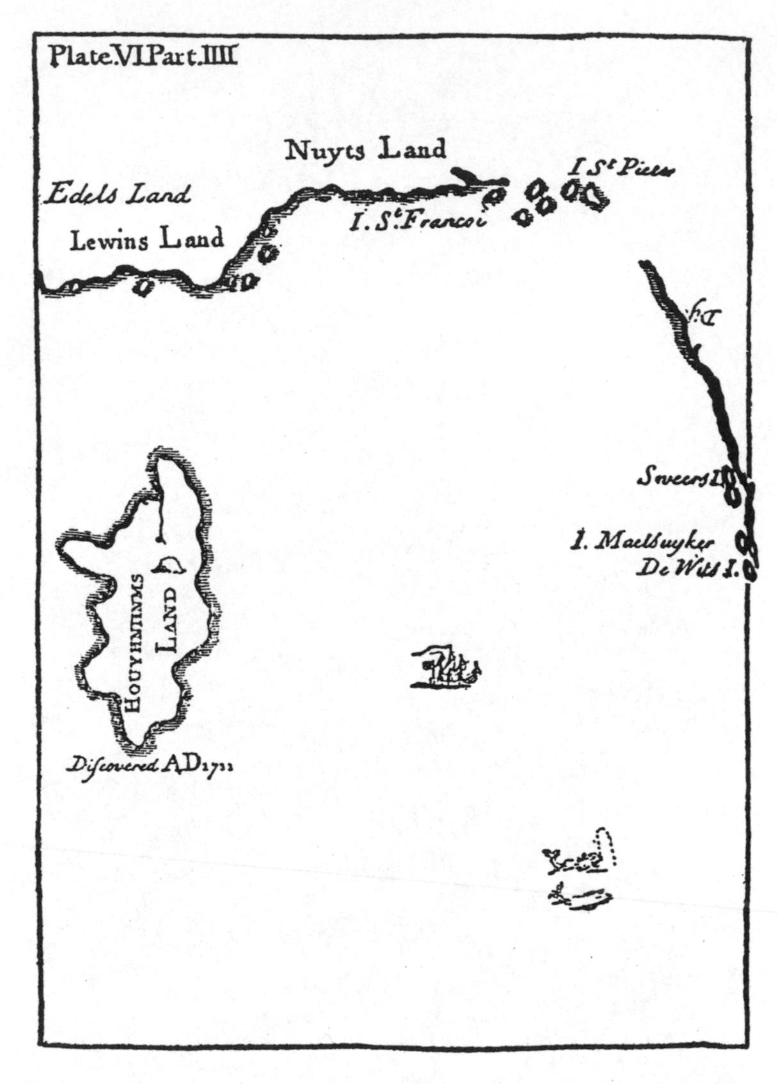

Gulliver's fourth voyage takes him to the country of the Houyhnhnms (pronounced hwin'ms), intelligent horses living in a society of peace, justice and goodwill. The only blot on the landscape is the subject race of 'Yahoos', who look like brutalised versions of human beings and have all their worst characteristics. Gulliver is at first mistaken for a Yahoo. On Swift's map, the Houyhnhnms' island is positioned off southern Africa, roughly corresponding to Madagascar (though Madagascar is mentioned as a separate place in the story).

EXTRACT: THE SIMPLE LIFE OF THE HOUYHNHNMS

The Houyhnhnms don't need MONEY. *Nor do they lead a life of* INDULGENCE. *Each horse does what is necessary for society. They have a simple vegetarian diet. They are seldom ill. But Gulliver tells his master that humans are obsessed with getting more and more money. The horse is puzzled. What can the well-off find to spend their money on? 'The most costly meats and drinks,' Gulliver explains.*

HE DESIRED I would let him know what these costly meats were, and how any of us happened to want them. Whereupon I enumerated as many sorts as came into my head, with the various methods of dressing them, which could not be done without sending vessels by sea to every part of the world, as well for liquors to drink, as for sauces, and innumerable other conveniences. I assured him that this whole globe of earth must be at least three times gone round, before one of our better female Yahoos could get her breakfast or a cup to put it in. He said that must needs be a miserable country which cannot furnish food for its own inhabitants. But what he chiefly wondered at, was how such vast tracts of ground as I described should be wholly without fresh water, and the people put to the necessity of sending over the sea for drink. I replied that England (the dear place of my nativity) was computed to produce three times the quantity of food, more than its inhabitants are able to consume, as well as liquors extracted from grain, or pressed out of the fruit of certain trees, which made excellent drink, and the same proportion in every other convenience of life. But, in order to feed the luxury and intemperance of the males, and the vanity of the females, we sent away the greatest part of our necessary things to other countries, from whence in return we brought the materials of diseases, folly, and vice, to spend among ourselves. Hence it follows of necessity that vast numbers of our people are compelled to seek their livelihood by begging, robbing, stealing, cheating, pimping, forswearing, flattering, suborning, forging, gaming, lying, fawning, hectoring, voting, scribbling, stargazing, poisoning, whoring, canting, libelling, freethinking, and the like occupations: every one of which terms, I was at much pains to make him understand.

That wine was not imported among us from foreign countries, to supply the want of water or other drinks, but because it was a sort of liquid which made us merry by putting us out of our senses, diverted all melancholy thoughts, begat wild extravagant imaginations in the brain, raised our hopes, and banished our fears, suspended every office of reason for a time, and deprived us of the use of our limbs, till we fell into a profound sleep; although it must be confessed, that we always awaked sick and dispirited and that the use of this liquor filled us with diseases, which made our lives uncomfortable and short.

But beside all this, the bulk of our people supported themselves by furnishing the necessities or conveniences of life to the rich, and to each other. For instance, when I am at home and dressed as I ought to be, I carry on my body the workmanship of an hundred tradesmen; the building and furniture of my house employ as many more, and five times the number to adorn my wife.

I was going on to tell him of another sort of people, who get their livelihood by attending the sick, having upon some occasions informed his Honour that many of my crew had died of diseases. But here it was with the utmost difficulty that I brought him to apprehend what I meant. He could easily conceive that a Houyhnhnm grew weak and heavy a few days before his death, or by some accident might hurt a limb. But that nature, who works all things to perfection, should suffer any pains to breed in our bodies, he thought impossible and desired to know the reason of so unaccountable an evil. I told him we fed on a thousand things which operated contrary to each other; that we ate when we were not hungry, and drank without the provocation of thirst; that we sat whole nights drinking strong liquors without eating a bit, which disposed us to sloth, inflamed our bodies, and precipitated or prevented digestion.

EAT,

DRINK &

BE MISERABLE

CHRISTINA HARDYMENT

on the way greed fuels illness

Getting and spending we lay waste our powers.
William Wordsworth

THE HOUYHNHNMS, dignified equine advocates of the simple spartan life, whinnied in disgust and disbelief when Gulliver outlined the grosser excesses – and consequent miseries – of his own society. It confirmed them in their belief that he and his countrymen were closely akin to Yahoos, the wild men of their own woods and creatures of unlicensed greed rather than reason. Would a latterday Gulliver cast up on their shores manage to convince them otherwise?

I think not. The insatiable world of our own consumer-driven economy would appal them even more than the reckless greed of early Georgian England. Today it is not just a matter of circumnavigating the world in search of tea and porcelain for aristocrats. We import both luxury goods and basic necessities in huge quantities – and these days everybody wants them. John Bull's overcrowded little island has been living well beyond its means ever since it surrendered the vast colonies that originally tempted it to adopt its profligate lifestyle.

Walk round your local supermarket with objective eyes and ask yourself what it tells you about the way we live now. At every turn we are challenged by choices. Battalions of variegated loaves flank mountains of imported butters; yoghurts by the yard and hundreds of cheeses nudge phalanxes of exotic and out-of-season fruits. Even the humble egg is stacked sky-high in infinite variety: fresh, farm fresh, free-range, barn-fed, all sized and graded as accurately as bra-cups.

In hypnotised trances, the customers stack trolleys that are made larger every year, buying more food that they can eat or afford. Culinary skills are out; buying time is in. Vegetables are trimmed ready for the pot and priced up accordingly. Meat of all cuts and kinds stretches away in bloodied ranks: raw, cooked, casseroled, curried. Most of it is produced by treating animals with grotesque cruelty.

Larders and ice-chests once encouraged economy: preserving today's harvest for tomorrow's needs. Now we use fridge-freezers as pick-and-mix cabinets from which we take what we want when we want it. Leftovers may spend a statutory few days lurking limply in their recesses, but nobody eats them. Novelty and freshness are essential to our jaded palates.

Yet a recent survey revealed that we throw away a quarter of the exotic ready-made dishes we are seduced into purchasing – either after a moment's tasting or when it passes its sell-by date. That ingenious death sentence must be as invaluable to the food industry as the mustard left on the sides of plates reputedly was to Mr Colman. We no longer trust ourselves to judge quality, and thrift has vanished along with the three-penny bits on which it was once stamped. The word itself is now an unfamiliar coinage.

Despite the tons of food carted home, we eat a rapidly increasing number of our meals in public places, at three times the price they would have cost us at home. Here wastage is even worse. The Christian miracle of the loaves and fishes is blasphemously parodied in cities every Saturday night: after revellers from clubs and pubs reel away, the streets are paved with heaps of crumpled cartons, foul with ketchup and chewed chips. Half-finished hamburgers are gnawed at by the rats which are once more thriving in drains and cellars. Special vehicles have been designed to cope with this slurry of curries and kebabs: huge wheeled hoovers that swish hungrily over the pavements and gutters, mechanically gobbling up what purchasers were too drunk or too sated to eat.

Behind more exquisite eateries with fancy French names the story is the same: wall-to-wall wheelie bins stuffed with the detritus of half-consumed dinners. This gourmet wastage may be more hygienically handled, but it is in a sense even more gross. So much time, effort and money is spent on creating meals for diners who exert themselves so little during the day that they are barely hungry when they enter the restaurant.

Stomachs are by no means the only things we indulge to excess. Lotions and potions stretch away down the supermarket aisles, their infinitesimal variations indulging our pretensions to individuality. Once it was only women's hair that was dyed and frizzed and frazzled, women's bodies that were lavished with unguents. Now men have tripled the time they spend on 'personal hygiene', and buy perfumes and anti-perspirants, wrinkle-reducers and hair-restorers as enthusiastically as women.

Next door to the supermarkets stand warehouses stacked with toys, white goods, furnishings and hi-fi. All, like our clothes, are designed for today and not tomorrow, their styling subtly shifting to seem old-fashioned. Technological advances of dubious usefulness are fed into the system year by year to keep customers constantly covetous, ever eager to upgrade. Consumer society is predicated on discontent.

As a result, more and more of our energies have to be dedicated to coping with what we throw away. Cavalcades of heavy trucks rumble along to the ever-expanding rubbish tips, their mighty metal jaws mashing up in minutes enough food to nourish whole villages in Ethiopia. In a ghastly parody of our once great mining industry, excavators and bulldozers bury mouldering food, indestructible packaging, industrial effluent and scrapped motor cars into the ground – or, with scant understanding of the consequences, the sea.

Irony of ironies, in one of the wettest islands in the world, we have even taken to buying the water we drink. Taint of chlorine and fear of fluoride make humble tap water suspect. Naturally, our favourite brand of fizzy water is a French one – at three times the price of an indistinguishable British equivalent.

Water is not the only thing we drink. Like the Yahoos, we use alcohol to distract us from the realities we cannot bear too much of. But we don't merely drink it to excess. We have elevated it to a kind of religion, with temples, high priests and high priestesses all its own: grand masters and mistresses of gargling and spitting, who lace their libations with arcane mantras and have educated their noses to distinguish grape from grape, vineyard from vineyard – all in the name of refining intoxication into an art form. Off-licences have developed from discreet annexes at the side of public houses into mini-supermarkets in their own right; chains of profiteers pepper the high street with Aladdin's caves of alcohol.

Hardly surprising then that the young, eager to ape adult ways, are seduced by television advertisements rather better made than the programmes they pay for. They vie to vomit vodka and extra-strong lager, buy whisky galore. And cigarettes. Tobacco, its popularity wavering among the mature as their contemporaries die of lung cancer, has been reprocessed as youth culture. It's cool to smoke, not least because of the government health warning on the packets. Hamlet is better known as a cigarillo than as a play, and the smartest fags to be seen with are trademarked Death.

How do we finance lifestyles better than we can afford? By credit, hire purchase, self-styled 'easy payment schemes' that may take the waiting out of wanting but may also cost us up to half as much again and are blowing up into a balloon of credit of South Sea Bubble proportions. We mortgage our futures to pay for present pastimes and pleasures with a myopic impatience that beggars belief – and, in time, the borrower.

Why do we tolerate all this? Simple. Our economy relies on consumer spending, even if what we are buying is rubbish and destructive rubbish at that. The Treasury benefits to the tune of billions a year from VAT and customs and excise duties. What government would set free the geese that lay its golden eggs? Besides, it desperately needs the money to run the extensive medical services required to cope with the swathe of physical and psychological destruction that drunkenness, debt and depression carve across society.

Now, as in Swift's time, the obverse of greed and excess is sickness and death. Vaccination and antibiotics have eradicated the diseases that used to stop populations growing; gynaecology and geriatrics have succeeded in establishing undreamt-of survival rates for mothers and senior citizens. But obesity is on the increase. Car seats and armchairs come wider these days; whole clothes stores cater for the outsize customer. Bulimia and anorexia nervosa, once unknown aberrations, have become all too familiar registers of inarticulate protest, especially among the young. And can it be mere chance that cancer, the most dreaded of modern ills, is in itself characterised by insatiability: rogue cells that refuse to stop multiplying?

Our most recent attempt to sate this infinity of desire is the vainest of all vanities. We dream of miraculously defying the odds, of winning more money than we could ever hope to earn – or spend, for that matter – from a public lottery run by private profiteers. Millions of us stump up weekly. We are now more likely to play the lottery than to vote. I doubt if even Swift could have predicted that the famously calm and rational Britain, cradle of democracy and fair play, would have taken up the fantasy world of instant wealth with such extraordinary enthusiasm. Yet what more can we expect from a society which has so fine-tuned the art of being Yahoo?

CHRISTINA HARDYMENT is a social historian and journalist. Her most recent book was *SLICE OF LIFE: THE BRITISH WAY OF EATING SINCE 1945.*

Extract: Gulliver Explains the Legal System

In the country of the Houyhnhnms, Gulliver finds it hard to EXPLAIN *just why his English countrymen are any better than the brutal, quarrelsome, greedy Yahoos. His peace-loving master eventually says he has heard enough of Gulliver's tales of the glory of war. He asks him to explain what he meant when he mentioned 'law' and 'lawyers'. These are concepts* UNKNOWN *among the Houyhnhnms, who are governed by reason, not by law.*

I SAID there was a society of men among us, bred up from their youth in the art of proving by words multiplied for the purpose, that white is black, and black is white, according as they are paid. To this society all the rest of the people are slaves. For example, if my neighbour hath a mind to my cow, he hires a lawyer to prove that he ought to have my cow from me. I must then hire another to defend my right, it being against all rules of law that any man should be allowed to speak for himself. Now in this case I who am the right owner lie under two great disadvantages. First, my lawyer, being practised almost from his cradle in defending falsehood, is quite out of his element when he would be an advocate for justice, which as an office unnatural, he always attempts with ill-will. The second disadvantage is that my lawyer must proceed with great caution, or else he will he reprimanded by the judges, and abhorred by his brethren, as one that would lessen the practice of the law. And therefore I have but two methods to preserve my cow. The first is to gain over my adversary's lawyer with a double fee, who will then betray his client by insinuating that he hath justice on his side. The second way is for my lawyer to make my cause appear as unjust as he can, by allowing the

cow to belong to my adversary: and this, if it be skilfully done, will certainly bespeak the favour of the bench.

Now, your Honour is to know that these judges are persons appointed to decide all controversies of property, as well as for the trial of criminals, and picked out from the most dexterous lawyers, who are grown old or lazy, and having been biassed all their lives against truth and equity, are under such a fatal necessity of favouring fraud, perjury, and oppression, that I have known several of them refuse a large bribe from the

Yahoos, by the great 19th century French caricaturist Grandville, who specialised in blending human and animal features. (Mary Evans Picture Library)

side where justice lay, rather than injure the faculty, by doing any thing unbecoming their nature or their office.

It is a maxim among these lawyers, that whatever hath been done before may legally be done again: and therefore they take special care to record all the decisions formerly made against common justice and the general reason of mankind. These, under the name of precedents, they produce as authorities, to justify the most iniquitous opinions; and the judges never fail of directing accordingly.

In pleading they studiously avoid entering into the merits of the cause, but are loud, violent, and tedious in dwelling upon all circumstances which are not to the purpose. For instance, in the case already mentioned, they never desire to know what claim or title my adversary hath to my cow; but whether the said cow were red or black, her horns long or short, whether the field I graze her in be round or square, whether she was milked at home or abroad, what diseases she is subject to, and the like; after which they consult precedents, adjourn the cause from time to time, and in ten, twenty, or thirty years, come to an issue.

It is likewise to be observed, that this society hath a peculiar cant and jargon of their own, that no other mortal can understand, and wherein all their laws are written, which they take special care to multiply; whereby they have wholly confounded the very essence of truth and falsehood, of right and wrong; so that it will take thirty years to decide whether the field left me by my ancestors for six generations belongs to me, or to a stranger three hundred miles off.

In the trial of persons accused for crimes against the state the method is much more short and commendable: the judge first sends to sound the disposition of those in power, after which he can easily hang or save the criminal, strictly preserving all due forms of law.

Here my master interposing, said it was a pity that creatures endowed with such prodigious abilities of mind as these lawyers, by the description I gave of them, must certainly be, were not rather encouraged to be instructors of others in wisdom and knowledge. In answer to which I assured his Honour that in all points out of their own trade, they were the most ignorant and stupid generation among us, the most despicable in common conversation, avowed enemies to all knowledge and learning, and equally disposed to pervert the general reason of mankind in every other abject of discourse, as in that of their own profession.

NEVER *GO TO* LAW

MARCEL BERLINS *reckons that English justice has improved – up to a point*

HOW IS IT, asks Gulliver's Houyhnhnm master, that 'the law which was intended for *every* man's preservation should be any man's ruin?' The question is as perceptive and as important today as it ever was in Swift's time. The precise answers may have changed in their detail over the centuries, but the central accusation remains. Indeed, we have far fewer excuses for our failings in 1996 than the law-givers and the law administrators had at the beginning of the Georgian era. Those in command of the law in recent years have made promises they have not kept and awakened expectations they have not fulfilled. At least, at the beginning of the 18th century, not many expected justice from the legal system, and the poor expected nothing. The tragedy of the end of the 20th century is that so many have been let down and feel betrayed.

But let us start with the positive changes. Much of Swift's critique was founded on the belief that lawyers were fundamentally crooked or at least, if that is too strong an accusation, that they were able to be persuaded through their purses. Nowadays, 'To gain over my adversary's lawyer with a double fee, who will then betray his client...' is no longer an option. Barristers may well demand double, and treble fees from their clients, but it will be to do their best for them, and no offer of quadruple fees from the opponent will budge them from their loyalty. The English barrister is no longer bribable, Swift would find to his surprise and disappointment.

He would not, though, fail to recognise other aspects of the barrister's working life. Counsel still wear the same fancy dress and the same peruques. Progress in barristerial dress was halted when Queen Anne died. The Bar went into black mourning, and has never emerged. And still the lawyers talk with 'a peculiar cant and jargon of their own, that no other mortal can understand, and wherein all their laws are written.' It remains one of the scandals of our time that laws are still written in impenetrable English even though it has been shown beyond doubt, by a few who care, that those same laws can be drafted in a language everyone can understand. But if laws were made comprehensible, how much less work for the lawyers in interpreting them; and if barristers in court spoke with clarity in people's English how much quicker would proceedings take, how much lower the lawyers' fees. That wouldn't do.

It is still true – necessarily so – that the skill of advocates lies in being able to prove 'that white is black, and black is white'. How else would they be able to earn a living other than by trying to persuade a jury that their client in the dock is innocent, in spite of having been apprehended at three in the morning wearing a mask, and carrying a bag marked 'Swag' containing the family silver from a nearby house?

Many a litigant today would cap Swift's story of his disputed cow with equally frightening tales of justice going wrong, of homes being taken away from those who need them, of children removed from a loving parent, of businesses plunged into financial ruin.

Those consequences happen not, as Swift would have it, because a lawyer, 'practised almost from his cradle to defending falsehood, is quite out of his element when he would be an advocate for justice,' but simply because advocacy and luck still play too great a part in the decisions reached by the courts. It is wrong that cases should be won or lost not because of their merits but because this advocate was better than that one, or because a truthful witness came over as hesitant in the witness-box, while the one who lied had a more convincing manner.

Our trial system – both criminal and civil – is adversarial. It is a contest between two sides, with the more persuasive side winning, which is too often not the same as the side that has right and justice in support. In criminal, as in civil cases, miscarriages of justice occur with frightening regularity. It is not a system aimed at getting at the truth of the issue but at playing the game better than the opponent.

The umpires in the game, the judges, are still largely chosen from the 'most dexterous lawyers' though, happily, no longer from those 'grown old or lazy... biassed all their lives against truth and equity... favouring fraud, perjury and oppression.' Our judges today are neither susceptible to bribes, nor feel any allegiance to dishonesty over rectitude. Nor, when faced with an important decision, do they telephone the government to find out which side they should be on.

On judges, Swift is at his most wrong. The standard of the English Judiciary is not just incomparably higher than in his time, but far higher than even 25 years ago, Most of the silly, prejudiced, sexist, crusty, drunk, remote, arrogant, lazy and stupid judges have left the bench; their replacements are altogether more able, and more or less in touch with the real world.

Yet the method of picking the High Court judiciary is still medieval; the choice of one man, the Lord Chancellor, albeit after taking soundings from the senior judiciary. The trouble is that those private chats tend to throw up candidates very like the judges doing the recommending. They will be male, and the kind of chaps who fit in. Not many women do. Fewer than six per cent of senior judges are women (though Swift, of course, took for granted a constant figure of nought per cent); none are black. It's not that the current higher judiciary is awful; but it could be so much better. Lower down in the hierarchy, at the circuit judge level and below, the strain of finding people of ability begins to show.

Judges are still, as Swift recorded caustically, tied to the dead weight of precedent. Good judges are forced to follow the decisions of bad judges; the law compels them to produce precedents 'as authorities to justify the most iniquitous opinions.' What has changed is that the judges now do so reluctantly, not enthusiastically.

The outstanding fault with the law today lies not with the judges, or with bad advocates – though there are disgracefully too many of them – but with the system in which they have to work. Gulliver's Houyhnhnm master made the point that the law was intended for *every* man's preservation. Law is supposed to be available to all citizens, for their protection. If only an elite (whether through money or connections) can make use of its facilities, it becomes a sham and an affront to a democratic society. It was a compatriot of Swift's who, a century ago, pointed out that, in England, justice is open to all, like the Ritz Hotel. Lord Justice Sir James Mathew's barb stung the English, and remained a niggle in the national legal psyche at a time when the English system of justice was being boasted of as the best in the world – which it was, for a lucky few.

After the second world war, the introduction of legal aid meant, for the first time, that the less well off could claim state money with which to fight their legal battles, and almost everyone charged with a serious crime would have the right to legal representation on the state. By the late 1970s nearly 80 per cent of households in England and Wales were eligible for civil legal aid. The figure is now less than 50 per cent, and declining. Treasury expenditure cuts are gobbling away at people's entitlement to enter the portals of justice. For those who are neither very rich, nor so poor as to qualify for state aid, going to law is an unattainable dream.

Our civil legal system is over-complex, time-consuming, riddled with delays and costly beyond reason. A good solicitor in London can charge £300 an hour, and an inexperienced, mediocre one £150. In 1995 some 20,000 clients were unhappy enough with the service they received from their solicitors to complain formally to the inefficient complaints body that usually failed to satisfy their grievances. A dozen or more barristers earn upward of three quarters of a million a year; and £300,000 is now commonplace. A week-long High Court trial can cost £100,000. Small wonder that people denied legal aid are unable to contemplate going to law, however sound their claim. A recent reform allowing lawyers to be paid only if their client wins the case is too cautious to make a big difference.

Swift feared that the dispute over his cow would take 30 years to resolve, quicker than Dickens's interminable case of Jarndyce versus Jarndyce in Bleak House. Delays are not of 30 years duration today; but they are outrageous nevertheless. Simple cases may take years to come to finality, because of unnecessarily complicated procedures which allow lawyers the greatest latitude, and countless opportunities to dabble in obscure procedural niceties – at the expense, of course, of the client.

There is reform in the wind. The law lord, Lord Woolf, has radical plans to improve the service of justice, to make it cheaper, quicker, easier, and above all more accessible to the ordinary person. But already his ideas are being undermined by the holders of the national purse-strings. Spending money on the law, the politicians in power have decided, does not win a single vote in an election. We are doomed to a legal system which works only in parts, to which only some people have access, in which the professionals are of high calibre only some of the time.

Swift realised then the great truth which is still the great truth today. Law is not justice, nor justice law. If we are lucky, the two travel towards each other and occasionally merge. During bad times – Swift's times – they stay obdurately apart. Today, the law 'intended for *every* man's preservation' rarely achieves that aim. Perhaps 'man's ruin' occurs not as frequently as it once did; but far too often for us to be too proud of the English legal system of 1996.

MARCEL BERLINS presents the Radio Four programme *LAW IN ACTION*. He is the author, with Clare Dyer, of *THE LAW MACHINE*.

THE LIFE & TIMES OF *JONATHAN* SWIFT

It was a difficult time in which to be sceptical, satirical or in any way detached from the prevailing orthodoxy. Swift lived through the years when much of what we now think of as Britain was being created, often with great bitterness and bloodshed.

The heart of that idea was that Britain should be an independent Protestant state. The fear of a return of papal authority can perhaps best be understood by thinking of it as similar, in its own day, to the British fear of German domination (by the Kaiser or by Hitler) in the two world wars. Or to the West's fear of ideological subversion by communist Russia.

The battle for a Protestant independent Britain veered between cold war and hot war. The hot war was usually waged against the Roman Catholic nations of France or Spain. In the cold war, internal enemies (those who held to their Catholic beliefs) were penalised. The Irish Catholics were seen – not wrongly – as offering a possible jumping-off point for a foreign enemy. They were relentlessly crushed. Much of the population was driven into poverty to sustain the incomes of the (mostly English) landlords.

Fears of what might happen if the Protestant dispensation was overthrown were not just scare stories. The horrors of religious warfare, and the murder and torture of Protestant believers, in France, Germany and the Low Countries, were not far in the past. Hence, also, the recurrent determination to have a Protestant monarch on the English/British throne. A quest not finally settled till George of Hanover became King.

This time of political turmoil was also a time of great voyages of discovery, and of scientific invention. Isaac Newton put forward his theory of gravity in 1687. He was President of the Royal Society from 1703 till his death in 1727. But as his mockery of the inhabitants of Laputa shows, Swift was as sceptical of scientific progress as of most other things he observed. **PB**

(Mary Evans Picture Library)

CHRONOLOGY

1667: JONATHAN SWIFT born in Dublin after death of lawyer father.

1668: 'Kidnapped' by family nurse and taken by boat to Whitehaven. Stays with her for three years.

1673: *Parliament passes Test Act, to keep Roman Catholics out of public office.*

1674-78: Swift educated at boarding school in Kilkenny and at TRINITY COLLEGE, Dublin.

1678: *Alleged Popish Plot uncovered in London. Various panic measures follow.*

1685: *Charles II dies. Roman Catholic brother, James II, succeeds to throne. Tries to restore dominant position of Catholic religion (and papal authority) in England. Driven into exile in 1689.*

1689: Swift becomes secretary to his first patron, SIR WILLIAM TEMPLE, in England. Starts to write poetry. *William III, Dutch head of state and a Protestant, becomes King of England, ruling jointly with James II's daughter, Mary. Bill of Rights protects parliamentary rule. In Ireland, rebellion in favour of James II, who rules for a while as King in Dublin. Northern Protestants declare for William. Protestant Londonderry besieged by Catholics for 105 days. (This is where the Ulster 'troubles' begin.)*

1690: *William defeats James at the BATTLE OF THE BOYNE.*

1694: Angry at lack of advancement, Swift goes back to Ireland, is ordained a minister of the Church of England, but soon returns to work with Temple. Meets Esther Johnson, then eight years old, who may have been Temple's illegitimate daughter. As 'STELLA' she becomes the subject of many of his poems.

1697: Writes first major satire, *THE BATTLE OF THE BOOKS.*

Top: The Pope burnt in effigy at Temple Bar c.1670.
Middle: Sir William Temple. (Mary Evans Picture Library) Bottom: The Battle of the Boyne. (Hulton Deutsch)

1699: Returns to Ireland after Temple's death. Takes up a post as clergyman again, though with few duties. Is often in London where he meets all the writers of the day.

1701-13: *War with France. Duke of Marlborough, victor of Battle of Blenheim, best-known general.*

1702: *Queen Anne succeeds to throne.*

1704: Swift finally publishes *The Battle of the Books*, together with *A Tale of a Tub*, his satire on 'corruption in religion and learning.'

1708: Swift begins a series of pamphlets on church questions, starting with the ironic *ARGUMENT AGAINST ABOLISHING CHRISTIANITY*. Many other pamphlets and satirical poems follow.

1710: Switches political support from Whigs to TORIES (in modern terms, from left to right, but not a precise analogy). Writes pamphlets in favour of ending the war. Begins his intimate *JOURNAL TO STELLA*, written partly in baby language but also chronicling current events.

1713: Becomes Dean of St Patrick's cathedral in Dublin. (English positions withheld because of objections to his satires.) Spends most of his income on local charities.
Much loved by local people.
A Tory government ends the war with France. As part of the peace treaty Gibraltar becomes British.

1716: *Queen Anne dies. Protestant King of Hanover brought over from Germany to English throne, as George I (direct ancestor of present queen). Whigs return to power. No jobs for Tories.*

1716: Swift may have secretly married Stella in IRELAND. But they never live together, and he nearly always sees her in the presence of a third party. From 1708 to 1723, he is also closely involved with another woman, Esther Vanhomrigh.

Top: Esther Johnson ('Stella'). Bottom: George I. (Mary Evans Picture Library)

1721: *Robert Walpole, a Whig, becomes first politician to be designated Prime Minister. Rules mainly through bribery, but his consistent policy is to keep Britain out of foreign wars.*

1724: Swift writes increasingly in defence of Ireland against social and economic injustices, but with no result.

1726: Makes last visit to London. Publishes *GULLIVER'S TRAVELS.* An immediate success.

1728: Stella dies. Swift continues to write poems and pamphlets till disabled by consequences of Ménière's Disease (ear infection, causing dizziness and nausea, from which he suffered for most of his life).

1729: Publishes the satirical pamphlet, *A Modest Proposal*, suggesting that, given English policies, the only way to bring prosperity back to the Irish is for their children to be fattened up for sale as food.

1742: *After 21 years as Prime Minister, Robert Walpole resigns. His career is ended by an unsuccessful war with Spain (which he opposed): the famous war of Jenkins's Ear.*

1745: Swift dies and is buried beside Stella in St Patrick's cathedral. He composed his own epitaph (in Latin). A translation reads:

'The body of Jonathan Swift, Doctor of Sacred Theology, dean of this cathedral church, is buried here, where fierce indignation can no more lacerate his heart.
Go, traveller, and imitate, if you can, one who strove with all his strength to champion liberty.'

Top: *Walpole (left) in the House of Commons.* (Mary Evans Picture Library)
Middle: *Merchants, led by Jenkins (with severed ear), confront Walpole.* (Hulton Deutsch)

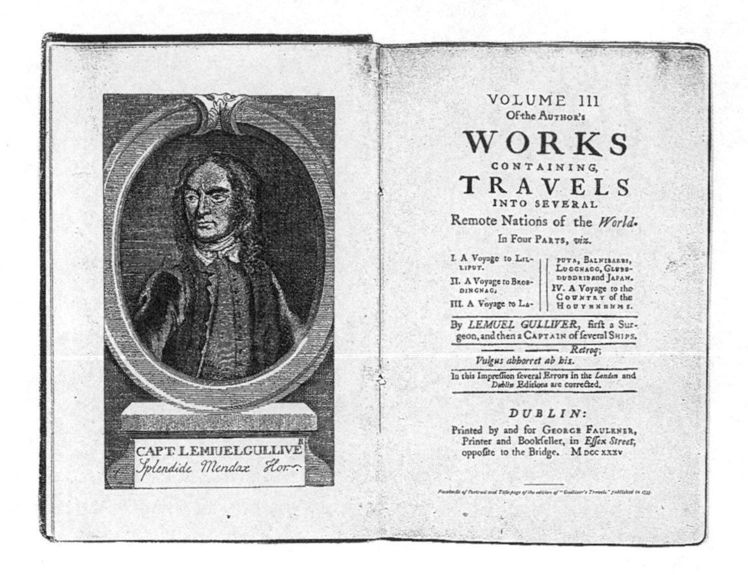

CAPT. LEMUEL GULLIVER
Splendide Mendax Hor.

VOLUME III
Of the AUTHOR's
WORKS
CONTAINING,
TRAVELS
INTO SEVERAL
Remote Nations of the *World*.
In Four PARTS, *viz.*

I. A Voyage to LILLIPUT.
II. A Voyage to BROBDINGNAG.
III. A Voyage to LAPUTA, BALNIBARBI, LUGGNAGG, GLUBBDUBDRIB and JAPAN.
IV. A Voyage to the COUNTRY of the HOUYHNHNMS.

By *LEMUEL GULLIVER*, first a Surgeon, and then a CAPTAIN of several SHIPS.

—— *Retroq;*
Vulgus abhorret ab his.

In this Impression several Errors in the *London* and *Dublin* Editions are corrected.

DUBLIN:
Printed by and for GEORGE FAULKNER, Printer and Bookseller, in *Essex Street*, opposite to the Bridge. MDCCXXXV

BOOKS

GULLIVER'S TRAVELS has never been out of print since it was published. Among the current versions are the Penguin Classics, Oxford World Classics and Everyman Library editions. Some of Swift's poems, including the scurrilous '*A BEAUTIFUL YOUNG NYMPH GOING TO BED*' and the ironic '*VERSES ON THE DEATH OF DR SWIFT*' are in *The New Oxford Book of 18th Century Verse*, edited by Roger Lonsdale. *THE WRITINGS OF JONATHAN SWIFT*, edited by RA Greenberg and WB Piper, brings together *Gulliver's Travels*, a selection of other prose pieces (including *A Modest Proposal)*, poems and critical comments.
It is published by WW Norton in its Norton Critical Edition series. For the general historical background, the best book is Professor Linda Colley's *BRITONS: FORGING THE NATION 1707-1837*
All the above are in paperback, apart from the Everyman edition, which is a high-quality cheap hardback.

FILMS

All the English language versions listed here are entitled *GULLIVER'S TRAVELS* (which usually meant just the Lilliput voyage), unless otherwise stated.
Other versions include the Spanish *LOS VIAJES DE GULLIVER.*

Facsimile of portrait and title page from the 1735 edition. Swift added the teasing motto 'Splendide Mendax' to this edition. It is a quotation from the Roman poet, Horace, and translates as 'magnificently untrue'.

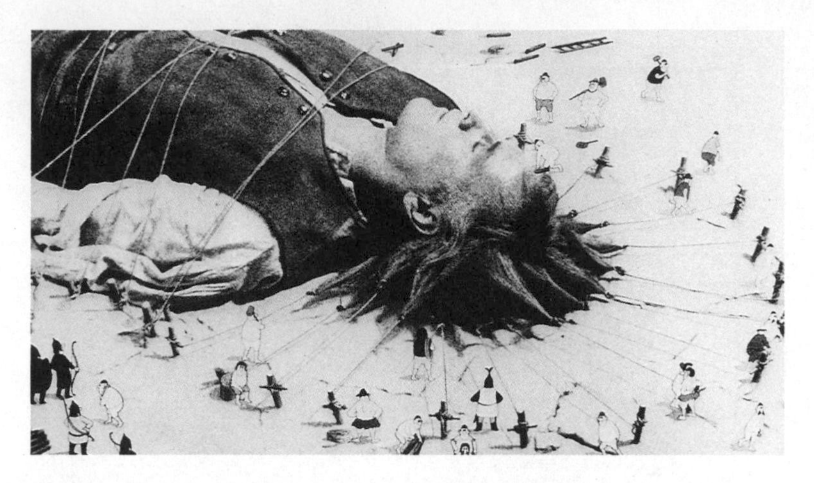

1939: Animated version by Max and Dave Fleischer. Gabby, the comic night-watchman who finds Gulliver on the beach, was popular enough to go on to star in his own series of short films.

1960: *The Three Worlds of Gulliver*. Live action version directed by Jack Sher. Ingenious trick shots.

1977: Actors (Richard Harris as Gulliver) and animation, directed by Peter Hunt. Low budget.

1979: Animated version by Hanna-Barbera, better known for the Flintstones.

1982: *Gulliver's Travels in Lilliput*. Live action, directed by Barry Letts. Made for BBC-TV.

1996: Live action version from Jim Henson Productions, broadcast on Channel 4, directed by Charles Sturrock. Actors and special effects. Includes all four voyages.

VIDEOS

The Jim Henson Productions film, broadcast on Channel 4 at Easter 1996, is available on video from May 1996. The Fleischer version (1939) is on video (sometimes listed as *The Story of Gulliver's Travels)* and is occasionally televised. It is based on only a few of the Lilliput incidents, and is often very sugary, but it is the best of the early films. Of the rest, the Peter Hunt (1977) and Hanna-Barbera (1979) versions are also currently on video.

Richard Harris as Gulliver in the 1977 version, directed by Peter Hunt. (BFI)